Queensland's Contribution to the Development of British New Guinea

PAUL DILLON

ABOUT THE AUTHOR

Paul Dillon is a Sunshine Coast based author of *Frederick Walker, Commandant of the Native Police*, Connor Court Publishing, Brisbane 2018; *The Murder of John Francis Dowling and the Massacre of 300 Aborigines*, Connor Court Publishing, Brisbane 2019; *Inside the Killing Fields Hornet Bank, Cullin-la-Ringo & The Maria Wreck*, Connor Court Publishing, Brisbane 2020; *Queensland Native Police, The First Twenty Years*, Brisbane, 2020; *The Irvinebank Massacre*, Connor Court Publishing, Brisbane 2021; *Fraser Island Massacre Vrai ou Faux*, Connor Court Publishing, Brisbane 2022; *Bêche-de-mer and the Binghis*, Brisbane, 2022; *The History of Bêche-de-mer Fishing in Queensland Waters and Adjacent Islands*, Connor Court Publishing, Brisbane 2023; *Dispela Kantri Bilong Mi, Nau! Queensland Annexes New Guinea*, Brisbane, 2023; and *Red Centre, Dead Centre, The True Story of Peter Falconer, Austin Macauley Publisher*, London 2019.

He holds a Bachelor of Arts degree from the Australian National University. Paul joined the Commonwealth Public Service in 1965. On 23 May 1986, he was called to the Bar of New South Wales and practised as a barrister in the Criminal Division of the superior courts of Queensland as counsel for the defence.

Sketches on the Fly River. (1885). Melbourne: Alfred Martin Ebsworth.

Queensland's Contribution to the Development of British New Guinea

Published in 2023 by Connor Court Publishing Pty Ltd

Copyright © Paul Dillon

All rights reserved. No part of this book may be reproduced or transmitted in any form or by any means, electronic or mechanical, including photo copying, recording or by any information storage and retrieval system, without prior permission in writing from the publisher.

Connor Court Publishing Pty Ltd
PO Box 7257
Redland Bay QLD 4165
sales@connorcourt.com
www.connorcourt.com

Printed in Australia

ISBN: 9781922815880

Front Cover Photograph: The Bulletin, Vol. 1 No. 4, 9 June 1883. How one Australian artist in 1883 dramatically depicted the annexation of New Guinea.

Front Cover Design: Maria Giordano

CONTENTS

Foreword 7

Preface 9

1 — The Political Evolution of British New Guinea 11
2 — Assessment 57
3 — Compare and Contrast 93
4 — Postscript 97

Table 1 — Marine Incidents 114

Bibliography 117

Foreword
by
Geoffrey Blainey

Living on the Sunshine Coast, Paul Dillon has devoted his time since 2018 to research on violent aspects of the colonial history of Queensland and the nearer tropical islands. Amongst his ten books are investigations into Queensland's frontier conflict, and to massacres that are well known or little known. Unlike several of the "black-armband historians" whom he analyses, he investigates the massacres of Europeans as well as the massacres of Aboriginals. Lately he has focussed on trade, missionary endeavours, bloodshed and politics on the tropical coastlines and seas just beyond mainland Queensland.

Dillon's latest book investigates, with keen attention to detail, colonial Queensland's role in the development of British New Guinea. It narrates the annexation, in parliament house in Brisbane, of the outer islands of Torres Strait after the arrival in 1871 of the London Missionary Society. It reveals the rising importance of Torres Strait and its international steamship traffic, the contest with Germany in 1883 for the easterly or non-Dutch portion of New Guinea and the attractive islands of New Britain and New Ireland. Without the determination of Queensland, Britain would never have set up a government house at Port

Moresby in 1888. Dillon reminds us that, in the eyes of some major politicians, the nearer parts of New Guinea were almost as essential as Tasmania. In essence, "New Guinea and the adjacent groups of Pacific Islands must form part of the future Australian nation."

It is especially Dillon's skill in weighing evidence, and in cross-examining long-dead witnesses, that makes him a historian worth reading. That he ventures into new territory is a bonus.

PREFACE

I began with the idea that I would write a complete history of marine incidents in Queensland waters and adjacent islands that involved indigenous elements. When first looked at, this seemed straightforward enough.

However, when the colony of Queensland is examined, it might be noted that Queensland not only dealt with Aboriginals and Chinese on the mainland of the colony but also imported Pacific Islanders on work permits; and expanded its colonial borders to include another aboriginal group called Torres Strait Islanders, and further still annexed part of an adjacent country, ultimately known as British New Guinea and involved itself in the administration of this group of people. As a consequence, the work became far too extensive to reduce to a book of even 500 pages.

Consequently, I divided the project into three parts: Aboriginals of the mainland and Torres Strait Islanders, Papuans, and Pacific Islanders.[1] The research involving the first group produced an extensive range of data that revealed 95 marine incidents involving Australian and Torres Strait indigenous elements. This study produced a manuscript of 103,600 words, which was privately published for

---

1 Indigenous means for these purposes any aboriginal native of Australia, Torres Strait, Papua, New Guinea, Pacific Islands & South Sea Islands; commonly known as Aborigines, Torres Strait Islanders, Papuans, Kanakas, Polynesians & South Sea Islanders.

a limited academic audience entitled, *Bêche-de-mer and the Binghis*.[2] An abridged and revised edition of this work was published under the title of *The History of Bêche-de-mer Fishing in Queensland Waters and Adjacent Islands*.[3]

The second area of study involved Papuan elements; this again produced an impressive collection of data which when refined and analysed resulted in an equally extensive manuscript of 115,000 words. This document was also privately published for a limited academic audience entitled, *Dispela Kantri Bilong Mi, Nau! Queensland Annexes New Guinea*.[4]

The third area of study, marine incidents in Queensland waters and adjacent islands involving Pacific Islander elements, is still under study.

The following pages of this book represent an abridged and revised edition of the original manuscript of *Dispela Kantri Bilong Mi, Nau!* without the inclusion of individual case studies.

---

2 ISBN: 978-0-9946381-4-4, Printed by InHouse Publishing www.inhousepublishing.com.au
3 The History of Bêche-de-mer Fishing in Queensland Waters and Adjacent Islands, Connor Court Publishing, Brisbane, 2023.
4 ISBN: 978-0-9946381-5-1, Printed by InHouse Publishing www.inhousepublishing.com.au

1

THE POLITICAL EVOLUTION OF BRITISH NEW GUINEA

The island of New Guinea lies approximately between the equator and 12 degrees South latitude and between 130 and 169 degrees East longitude. In a 1660 treaty, the Dutch East India Company (VOC) recognised the Sultanate of Tidore's supremacy over the Papuan people, the inhabitants of New Guinea. In 1872 Tidore recognised Dutch sovereignty and granted permission to the Kingdom of the Netherlands to establish an administration in its territories whenever the Netherlands Indies authorities would want to do so. This allowed the Netherlands to legitimise a claim to the New Guinea area. The Dutch established the 141st meridian of East longitude as the eastern frontier of their territory.[5]

To the south of New Guinea lies the continent of Australia. The Australian land mass was occupied by the Kingdom of Great Britain and Ireland as a penal colony, known as New South Wales, from 26 January 1788. The colony was formally proclaimed by Governor Phillip on 7 February 1788 at Sydney and extended from the 135th meridian East between the latitudes of 10°37' S. and 43°39' S. On

---

5 https://en.wikipedia.org/wiki/Dutch_New_Guinea & Sydney Morning Herald 14 January 1885 p 7.

10 December 1859, a proclamation was read by George Bowen, the first Governor of Queensland, formally establishing Queensland as a separate colony from New South Wales. By 10 October 1878, the northern boundary of Queensland included the whole of the Torres Strait, effectively drawing the border between New Guinea and Queensland at the shoreline of New Guinea with the Queensland western boundary at the 138th meridian of East longitude.[6]

This meant that all the land in New Guinea east of the 141st meridian of longitude including the islands between the equator and the Torres Strait was available for annexation by any country. British New Guinea was a colonial country constructed from that available existing land mass, having no regard for the indigenous geography as understood by the occupying autochthons, ignoring original land borders and dividers and/or tribal homelands or traditional territories. By 1883, the island of New Guinea was completely occupied and colonised, as the map below shows.

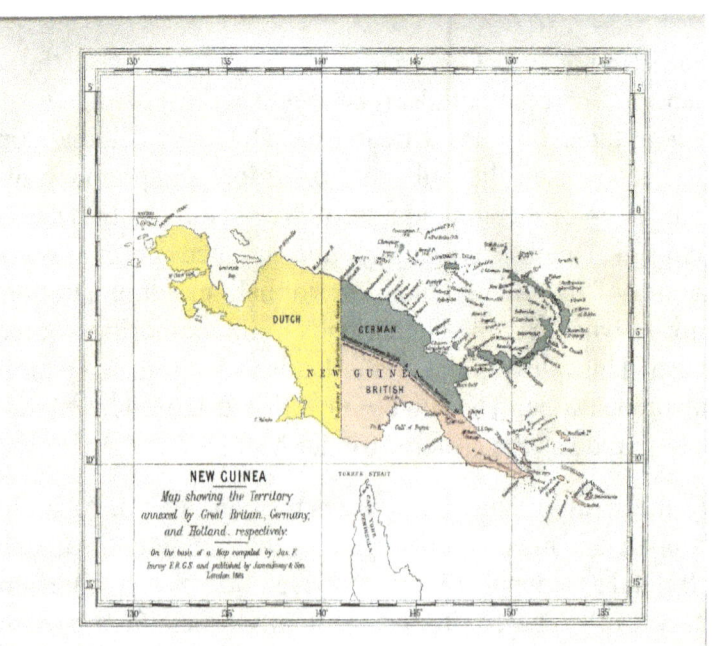

---

6   Supplement to the Queensland Government Gazette of 21 June 1879 No. 108 p 1379 & GG Vol. XXV.] 21 July 1879 [No.10 p 143.

THE PACIFIC ISLANDERS' PROTECTION ACTS, 1872 AND 1875 (IMPERIAL).

The Imperial Kidnapping Act took effect on the high seas on and from 27 June 1872. Thus, giving the Royal Navy power to intercept and seize all British shipping carrying Pacific islanders that were in breach of the Act. The adoption of the Kidnapping Act by the colony of Queensland meant the Act also applied and operated within Queensland waters on and from 31 August 1872.

On 8 March 1875, the Earl of Carnarvon presented a Bill to the House of Lords to amend the Kidnapping Act of 1872. On 16 March 1875, in moving the second reading, he said that the amendments were of a housekeeping nature.[7]

On 4 May 1875, he moved a further amendment to the Pacific Islanders' Protection Bill, to insert a new Clause 6 to empower Her Majesty to exercise jurisdiction over British subjects in islands of the Pacific Ocean not within the jurisdiction of any civilised Power; by Order-in-Council to create and constitute the office of High Commissioner in and over such islands, with authority to make regulations for the government of British subjects therein; to erect a Court of Justice for British subjects with civil, criminal, and Admiralty jurisdiction, corresponding with the authority of the High Commissioner; giving power to Her Majesty in Council to make ordinances for the government of British subjects being within these islands; and conferring on the High Commissioner certain powers.[8] The upshot of this legislation was not the acquisition of territory but the control and regulation of British Subjects within a defined geographical area of the Pacific Ocean known as the British Western Pacific Territories. Furthermore, the 1875 Act contained a saving clause to the effect that the rights of the indigenous tribes would be protected.[9]

---

7   HL Deb 8 March 1875 vol 222 c 1388.
8   HL Deb 04 May 1875 vol 224 cc 2-3. See clause 6 of the Pacific Islanders Protection Act 1875 (Imperial).
9   Section 7 of the Pacific Islanders' Protection Acts, 1872 and 1875.

ANNEXATION OF NEW GUINEA.

Sydney, May 19, 1875. A large deputation of merchants and others interviewed the Premier, Mr. John Robertson, asking him to urge upon the Home Government the necessity of annexation of New Guinea by Great Britain. The Premier expressed himself in favour of annexation and promised to consult his colleagues with the view of forwarding the representations of the deputation to the Secretary of State for the Colonies.[10]

On 3 June 1875, Sir Hercules Robinson, Governor of NSW, wrote to Carnarvon, the Secretary of State for the Colonies enclosing a Cabinet Minute by Mr. Robertson, the Premier, advocating the immediate annexation not only of the magnificent Island of New Guinea but of the Islands of New Britain, New Ireland, etc. & etc.[11]

On 17 June 1875 Mr. Douglas, Premier of Queensland, moved that the House consider an address to Her Majesty, relating to the Polynesian, Melanesian, and Papuan Archipelagos. Mr. Douglas said the annexation of New Guinea would be a very gradual process-anything like a sudden and forcible annexation could not be thought of. There had already been a connection between our pearl fisheries and New Guinea. Some islanders from New Guinea, being employed in the trade of this colony, it seemed to him not unfitting to show that they took considerable interest in the matter. Queensland was more interested in it than any other of the Australian colonies; and, therefore, it was desirable to express that opinion in some such form as that now proposed by him. It was agreed, the address:

> We desire to express to Your Majesty the satisfaction we have felt at the course pursued by Your Majesty's Government in accepting the cession of the Fijian group of islands; and we would humbly express to Your Majesty our opinion that, for the extension of British interests, for the protection of Your Majesty's subjects now resident in or adjacent to New Guinea, and for the promotion of civilisation

---

10 Brisbane Courier 20 May 1875 p 2 & Sydney Morning Herald 20 May 1875 p 3 PROPOSED ANNEXATION OF NEW GUINEA.
11 QSA ID ITM7168 & Sydney Morning Herald 6 August 1875 p 9 PROPOSED ANNEXATION OF NEW GUINEA.

among the native population, it is desirable that the whole of that island and the adjacent islands, not at present occupied by any European power, should be taken possession of by Your Majesty, and brought under the protection of Your Majesty's Government.[12]

On 6 July 1875, Governor of Queensland, W. W. Cairns forwarded from each house of legislature an address to Her Majesty to the Earl of Carnarvon.

Adelaide, August 12. The South Australian Parliament proposed to memorialise the Queen in favour of annexing New Guinea; addresses on the subject were agreed to by both Houses.[13]

London, November 13. The representations of the respective Australian Governments, in favour of the annexation of New Guinea to the colonial possessions of Great Britain, were under the consideration of the Cabinet.[14]

Then on 13 January 1876, Carnarvon, the Secretary of State for the Colonies replied to the Queensland government observing that he had received similar communications from other Australasian colonies about further annexation whether in New Guinea or elsewhere in the Pacific, as follows:

2. The principal reasons which have been advanced for the extension of British sovereignty over New Guinea and other Islands of the Pacific may fairly be summed up as follows:

(1.) That their possession would be of value to the Empire and conduce especially to the peace and safety of Australia, the development of Australian trade, and the prevention of crime throughout the Pacific.

(2.) That the establishment of a Foreign Power in the neighbourhood of Australia would be injurious to British, and more particularly to Australian interests.

3. But it is urged that although primarily of importance to

---

12 Hansard LA 17 June 1875 p 498-502.
13 Brisbane Courier 28 August 1875 p 6.
14 Brisbane Courier 25 November 1875 p 2.

Australia, it is as an Imperial question that this annexation should be considered, and I am further led to understand that those Colonies which would derive most advantage, whether in a political or a commercial point of view, from this step, are of opinion that no part of its cost should be defrayed from colonial funds.

5. Your Ministers refer at some length to the facilities which would be given for repressing abuses and maintaining order by the establishment of British Sovereignty throughout the Islands. ... she has created by Imperial legislation adequate machinery for establishing and maintaining the authority of a High Commissioner over such places in the Pacific as it may from time to time seem expedient to bring under his jurisdiction. Your Advisers will in fact find that the 6th section of the *Pacific Islanders Protection Act, 1875* (passed since their minute was written) answers in effect most of the latter part of their suggestions. It will, under this Act, be in the power of Her Majesty's Government should they think fit, to bring within the control of the High Commissioner the places referred to by your Ministers as desirable for annexation. And it will thus be possible to punish crime, to supervise the local trade, and—it may perhaps be added—to learn by experience how far there are other places which it may be expedient or necessary to bring absolutely under British rule.

6. As, therefore, provision has been in the manner which I have explained, for the exercise of some authority over British subjects in the places under consideration, the principal if the only ground on which Her Majesty's Government could be pressed to come to so hasty a decision as is now urged, in favour of further extending the Queen's Sovereignty in the Pacific, would be the imminent probability of annexation of New Guinea by some Foreign State.[15]

---

15   QSA ID ITM7168.

HIGH COMMISSIONER FOR THE WESTERN PACIFIC.

On 13 August 1877, the Queen created the Western Pacific Order-in-Council of 1877 pursuant to the Pacific Islanders' Protection Acts 1872 and 1875, and by the Foreign Jurisdiction Acts 1843 to 1875, and appointed Sir Arthur Gordon, High Commissioner and Consul-General for the Western Pacific. The islands and places to which this Order extended and applied to were set out in the Order and were collectively referred to as the Western Pacific Islands. Among these islands and places were:

(3.) The part of the Island of New Guinea eastward of the 143rd meridian of longitude.

(4.) The Islands or Archipelago of New Britain and New Ireland.

(5.) The Louisiade Archipelago.[16]

Commodore Wilson writing on the High Commission for the Western Pacific to the secretary of the Admiralty on 5 July 1879 observed:

> The institution of this court is likely to have a great influence, either for good or bad, on trade in these seas. Its powers are great, but, after careful study of the order in Council, they appear to be mainly in one direction, viz., the protection of the native against the British subject; but it is not equally clear that it has any authority to punish the native for pillage or outrage on our countrymen.
>
> This is a serious matter to the Trader; he is presumably precluded from taking the law into his own hands and now carries arms for self-defence at a great risk. Allowing that every consideration is made for the position in which he finds himself in each case, the very fact of being summoned to appear before this tribunal at Fiji will alone suffice to ruin him, whether he be acquitted or not. Hitherto Traders have, to a great extent, protected themselves and fought their own way; certainly, ships of war are usually sent to visit the scenes of murder or massacre, but they can seldom do so until after the lapse

---

16 New South Wales Government Gazette 5 June 1878 [Issue No.166 (SUPPLEMENT)] p 2210. Disraeli's colonial policy: The creation of the Western Pacific High Commission, 1874–1877, Historical Studies: Australia and New Zealand Volume 9, Issue 35 (1960): 279-294.

of months when it is too late to save property or to strike with good effect. In such cases Traders have often combined and punished the aggressors, if not leniently, at all events, as a rule, justly; and so far less by help from HM Cruisers, than by their own prowess and hardihood, have they held their own amongst the savages of these islands. Now, should the master of a trading vessel resent the murder of his men, he is liable to be arraigned before the High Commissioner, and, no matter how excusable or manly his conduct may have been, it being illegal, he will, as has been done in the case of others, be severely punished.

It is not my wish or province to comment upon the duties or office of the court in question but I desire respectfully to submit that if her Majesty's Government makes it illegal for the Traders to protect themselves, in justice, suitable and sufficient protection should be afforded him, such protection cannot be furnished by the small squadron now kept on the station, comprising, as it does, some thousands of islands, peopled almost invariably by lawless savages and cannibals.[17]

PROPOSED GERMAN ANNEXATION OF NEW GUINEA.

On 13 December 1882, Frederick Young, Honorary Secretary to the Royal Colonial Institute of London sent a copy of the *Allgemeine Zeitung*, of 27 November 1882 to Mr. Archer, Queensland Agent-General reminding him of the Institute's long history of promoting the annexation of New Guinea and asking him to draw to the Queensland government's attention the contents of the magazine recommending the German Government annex and colonise New Guinea. On 15 December 1882, Archer sent a copy of the magazine *Allgemeine Zeitung*, of 27 November 1882, to the Colonial Secretary.[18]

The *Brisbane Courier* of 15 February 1883 picked up an article that had been published by the *Sydney Morning Herald* covering the *Allgemeine Zeitung*, of 27 November 1882, which contained a long description of New Guinea and finished by urging that the

---

17 Item 04-Islands of the Western Pacific. Commodore Wilson to Secretary of Admiralty, PMB_1214-04.pdf.
18 QSA ID ITM7168.

island should be annexed by Germany, as the foundation of a future German colonial kingdom. The article went on to say:

> ... that the German nation should annex that somewhat mysterious yet attractive island, with a view of thereby laying the foundations of a German colonial empire. A proposal of this kind is not without interest for Australians, and we hardly fancy that such a scheme would be carried out without our neighbours in Queensland, for instance, having something to say to it. Should the Germans undertake seriously to carry out this project, it would probably be a somewhat different affair from the New Ireland colonisation idea as carried out by the Marquis de Rays.[19]

THE ANNEXATION OF NEW GUINEA BY QUEENSLAND.

On 14 March 1883, the Governor of Queensland, A. E. Kennedy wrote to the Earl of Derby, Secretary of State for the Colonies, asking him to consider the enclosed letter dated 26 February 1883, and other papers on the annexation of New Guinea:

26 February 1883.

Sir A. E. Kennedy,

This Government (Queensland) is of opinion that the time has now arrived for reviving the subject of the annexation of New Guinea; not merely the extending of British Sovereignty over such portion of it as is not claimed by the Government of the Netherlands, but the including of such within the territorial jurisdiction of Queensland.

With regard to the general question of annexation, the Earl of Carnarvon's Despatch to Sir H. Robinson, dated 8 December 1875, still holds good, and with even greater force than at that period, viz.:

(1.) That the possession of New Guinea and adjacent islands would be of value to the Empire and conduce especially to the peace and safety of Australia, the development of Australian trade, and the prevention and punishment of crime throughout the Pacific.

(2.) That the establishment of a Foreign Power in the neighbourhood of Australia would be injurious to British, and more particularly to

---

19 Sydney Mail and New South Wales Advertiser 10 February 1883 p 253 & Brisbane Courier 15 February 1883 p 3.

Australian interests.

I may take for granted that Your Excellency is fully cognisant of various recent events which give evidence of the fact that the Pacific region generally is now attracting the attention of more than one civilised power, with the view to the establishment of centres of influence as well sources of profit; and especially to the accompanying letter from the Agent-General, covering a communication from the Honorary Secretary of the Colonial Institute, regarding a recent article in the *Allgemeine Zeitung* (a translation of which is attached), I am myself of opinion that the probability of the colonisation of New Guinea, or, at all events, the formal occupation of some favourable point on the island, by some other power than Great Britain, is very largely increased.

Should it be decided to annex New Guinea, the selection of Queensland as the colony under whose jurisdiction New Guinea should be placed shows through the increased facilities of communication, existing between Queensland and New Guinea. Among others, I may enumerate,

1st. The extension of telegraphic communication from Cooktown to Thursday Island.

2nd. The establishment of the Torres Strait Mail Service by the Government of Queensland.

3rd. The establishment of a Steam Mail Service between Thursday Island and Normanton.

4th. The appointment of Thursday Island as a station for one of the gunboats now being ordered by the Queensland Government.

And to these, I would add that Queensland (is) a natural source of responsibility for the safety and order of all settlements in Torres Strait.

In the event of the Imperial Government deciding upon the annexation of New Guinea to Queensland, the (Queensland) Government would also be prepared to recommend Parliament to grant the necessary appropriation for defraying the cost of settlement and maintaining, if necessary, an armed force for the defence of the settlers, in this way meeting the objection which seems to have determined Her Majesty's Government against taking action in the matter at the period of the previous correspondence. Thomas McIlwraith.

On 26 February 1883, McIlwraith, Premier sent the following telegram to the Agent-General for Queensland in London:

> Urge Imperial Government annex New Guinea to Queensland Reasons large increase steamer traffic through Torres Strait Population settled there require government Imperial coaling depôt established Danger to colonies if other powers take possession Queensland will bear expense of government and take formal possession on receipt of Imperial authority by cable Letters by mail.

At a meeting of the Executive Council at Government House on 15 March 1883, the Governor in Council approved the annexation of New Guinea, in the name of Her Majesty, of so much of the island as is not in possession of the Netherlands Government. By 20 March 1883, the Colonial Secretary had authorised and directed Henry M. Chester, Police Magistrate at Thursday Island to take formal possession of the whole of the island of New Guinea except for that portion in occupation of the Dutch, in Her Majesty's name and was further directed to do all in his power to conciliate the natives with a supply of usual trade.

On 13 April 1883, Thomas McIlwraith, Premier, advised the Governor, Sir A. E. Kennedy, that H. M. Chester on the 4th instant had taken possession in the name of Her Majesty of all that part of New Guinea and isles adjacent thereto lying between the one hundred and forty-first and the one hundred and fifty-fifth meridian of east longitude. He further suggested that in the event of a request for an explanation of this summary step, the governor should impress upon the Secretary of State for the Colonies that the Queensland Government had acted under the full belief that the matter was too urgent to wait for instructions from the Imperial Government. As the possession of this valuable territory depended on mere precedence in the formality of annexation, and as the Queensland Government had strong reason to believe in the possibility and even the probability of action by a foreign power, a contingency which could not but gravely affect the Australasian Dependencies of Great Britain, as tending not only to limit the range of their development but possibly also to imperil their safety, it was hoped that the Secretary of State would perceive that in the step taken by the Queensland Government, they have been guided by considerations of expediency, which justified their promptness in taking action in the matter.

The Aborigines' Protection Society wrote to the Earl of Derby about the Queensland Government for the annexation of New Guinea and urged the Home Government not to permit the island to be administered by the colonial authorities, but be made a Crown colony, directly subject to the Colonial Office. The letter also strongly animadverted upon outrages which it alleged had from time to time been committed by the Queensland police in their dealings with Queensland blacks.[20]

ANNEXATION OF NEW GUINEA — MINISTERIAL STATEMENT IN THE HOUSE.

The Premier (Sir T. McIlwraith) said:

> I have received a telegram from the Agent-General in London, which, I think, entails upon me the duty of making a sort of ministerial statement to the House. The telegram is as follows:
>
> June 3, 1883.
>
> Lord Derby in House last night disallowed annexation States the other Powers making settlement would not be viewed as friendly act Prepared to extend to New Guinea the power of High Commissioner Unable to obtain interview today.
>
> Hon. members will remember that a few days ago the Governor's Speech contained the following paragraph:
>
> For some time past the imminent danger of annexation by a Foreign Power of the adjacent island of New Guinea has caused my government much concern and uneasiness. Ultimately, it was determined by a formal act of annexation to establish permanently British claims to the possession of that country. Accordingly, that portion of New Guinea east of the one hundred and forty-first meridian and the adjoining islands up to the one hundred and fifty-fifth meridian were annexed on the fourth of April last. This action

---

20   Sydney Mail and New South Wales Advertiser 26 May 1883 p 974.

has not yet received the sanction of Her Majesty; but there can be no question that, however distasteful to some of our countrymen at home further extensions of territory may be, New Guinea and the adjacent groups of Pacific Islands must form part of the future Australian nation. The course taken by my government has, in my opinion, furnished the best possible security against future embarrassments, and I am happy to state has received the hearty endorsement of the several Australian Colonies. I may add that at the instance of the Victorian Government concerted action has been taken with the object of inducing Her Majesty's Government to annex those Islands in the Pacific whose interests are deemed in many respects identical with those of Australia.

That paragraph in the Speech was, I think, universally approved of by hon. members of the House. It had the hearty approval of the leader of the Opposition, the modest approval of the Ministers, and the approval of hon. members generally. The Speech was adopted without amendment, and an Address endorsing that paragraph amongst others was passed by the House. I do not wish to comment on the reasons given by either the Secretary of State for the Colonies, or by the Premier of Great Britain, for the course so inimical to the interests of Queensland and the other Australian colonies which the mother-country has thought fit to adopt on the present occasion. I merely wish to point out that so far as Queensland is concerned and the other colonies, too, as an accomplished fact. I question the legality of the decision of Mr. Gladstone when he says that the action was null and void. I believe that it was perfectly legal and that we were fully entitled to annex the island without the formal sanction of the Government of Great Britain. That is my opinion, and upon it, I have acted. At all events, I am sure that it is the desire of the people of Queensland and of all the Australian colonies that annexation should take place, and that no step should be left untaken that will bring about that result. That we shall ultimately succeed, I have not the slightest doubt.[21]

On 11 July 1883, the Secretary of State for the Colonies, Lord Derby, replied to Sir Arthur Kennedy's request on behalf of the Government of Queensland that the eastern portion of New Guinea, with the islands adjacent thereto, be annexed to Queensland:

Her Majesty's Government were unable to approve the proceedings of your government in this matter. It is well understood that the

---

21 Sydney Mail and New South Wales Advertiser 7 July 1883 p 35. Hansard LA 4 July 1883 p 89-91.

officers of a Colonial Government have no power or authority to act beyond the limits of their Colony, and if this constitutional principle is not carefully observed serious difficulties and complications must arise. It is therefore much to be regretted that your advisers should, without apparent necessity, have taken on themselves the exercise of powers which they did not possess.

3. The apprehension entertained in Australia that some foreign Power was about to establish itself on the shores of New Guinea appears to have been altogether indefinite and unfounded, and the inquiries which have been made by Her Majesty's Government have given them the strongest reasons for believing that no such step has been contemplated. Nor is there at the present time any sufficient ground for anticipating the early settlement on the shores of New Guinea of a white population from the Australasian Colonies which, in the absence of any established authority, would become a source of trouble and danger to the Colony.

4. Her Majesty's Government are, moreover, clearly of opinion that even if the time had arrived for asserting and exercising the Queen's authority and jurisdiction on the shores of the island, or on some portions of them, there would be no necessity or justification for including in these measures the whole of the vast territory to which the proclamation of the Queensland Government purports to apply.

5. If however, it had been shown that the extension of the Queen's sovereignty to the eastern portion of New Guinea has become necessary, the proposal that the territory so annexed should form part of the colony of Queensland would be open to strong objections. The Colony already comprises an immense extent of territory: the seat of Government is situated in the south, a thousand miles from the south-eastern point of New Guinea: it is practically governed by a Parliament which represents the white population, whose interests are altogether different from those of the races, aboriginal and imported, within the colony: and while I am aware of the difficulties with which the Colonial Government has had to contend in connexion with the labour traffic and other questions affecting native interests, the fact that those difficulties have not in all cases been successfully dealt with cannot be disputed, and has often of late been the subject of much comment. The Queensland Government is at present undertaking heavy charges and responsibilities in connexion with the settlement and development of its vast northern territory, which cannot be fully occupied for many years to come, and even if it could be reconciled with former precedents and sound general principles that the Imperial Government should devolve

upon any colony the duties incident to the establishment of British dominion in such a country as New Guinea, neither the time nor the circumstances would appear favourable for the assumption by the Queensland Government of the control of a large native population owning a territory not required, and, to a great extent at least, not suited for the occupation and labour of European settlers. It has been stated in the press that one reason for which some persons in Queensland desire the annexation of New Guinea is the facility which would thereby be afforded for obtaining a large supply of coloured labour for the sugar plantations without going beyond the limits of the colony. It is no doubt generally understood that the natives of New Guinea would not willingly accept or be suitable for labour engagements at a distance from their shores, but the fact that the suggestion has been made indicates a special difficulty which might present itself if the request of the Colonial Government were complied with.

6. Her Majesty's Government have not failed to give due attention to the representations made by the Governments of New South Wales, Victoria, and South Australia in support of the action taken by your government. Those Governments do not, as I understand, definitely endorse the proposal that the island should form part of Queensland, nor do they undertake to share the expenses which might be entailed by any attempt to govern it, but they express in general terms a desire that it should be brought under British rule and I trust the time is now not distant when the Australasian Colonies will effectively combine together and provide the cost of carrying out any policy which, after mature consideration, they may unite in recommending, and which Her Majesty's Government may think it right and expedient to adopt.

7. In the meantime, Her Majesty's Government are of opinion that they must continue to decline proposals for large annexations of territory adjacent to Australia, in the absence of sufficient proof of the necessity of such measures. In the case of New Guinea, there is already in existence a jurisdiction which may be made to suffice for immediate exigencies. The powers of the High Commissioner for the Western Pacific extend to that island, and if the Colony of Queensland, with or without assistance from other colonies, is prepared to provide a reasonable annual sum to meet the cost of placing one or more Deputies of the High Commissioner on the coast, Her Majesty's Government will be willing to take steps for strengthening the naval force on the Australian station, so as to enable Her Majesty's ships to be more constantly present than hitherto in that part of the Pacific. A protectorate thus gradually

established over the coast tribes would be capable of meeting the principal requirements of the case for some time to come and would be free from the grave objections to which, as I have shown, the course now urged upon Her Majesty's Government is open. Derby.[22]

Brisbane, 17 July 1883. At a meeting of the Executive Council, a memorandum by the Premier on the annexation of New Guinea was adopted and ordered to be transmitted to her Majesty's Government, and likewise to the Governments of all the Australian colonies. This document set forth the grounds on which the annexation was justified. It pointed out that the expense to be incurred need not be very great, because the Dutch, who also claim and hold a part of the island, go to no expense at all. What was needed was that New Guinea should not fall into the hands of any foreign power; and that some recognised authority should be created capable of dealing with lawless adventurers who might establish themselves on the island. As no difficulty was experienced in dealing with characters of this sort who had established themselves in the islands in Torres Strait when those islands had by proclamation been brought within the jurisdiction of Queensland, no similar difficulty need be apprehended if the mainland of New Guinea were proclaimed British territory.[23]

In the Commons of 18 August 1883, Mr. Gladstone, in answering a question of Mr. Ashmead-Bartlett about New Guinea, replied:

> I may repeat, what I think has been stated on the part of the Government before, that we have no reason whatever to apprehend any intention showing location on the part of any Foreign Government to make new territorial claims or establishments with respect to that Island. With regard to the direct Question of the hon. Gentleman, I conceive the position to be this—The matter was brought under our notice in connection with a particular proceeding on the part of the Government of Queensland; and the immediate question for us to consider was, whether we should confirm the so-called annexation of New Guinea—whether we should keep the question open for explanation in regard to that annexation, or whether we should decline altogether, and should annul the proceeding, and quash it by the authority of the Crown. It was the

---
22 https://www.parliament.vic.gov.au/papers/govpub/ VPARL1884No60.pdf
23 Sydney Mail and New South Wales Advertiser 21 July 1883 p 109.

last of these courses on which we decided, and that proceeding has been absolutely quashed and has no legal force whatever.[24]

THE INTER-COLONIAL CONVENTION OF 1883

The Inter-colonial Convention of 1883 was convened in Sydney on 28 November 1883. A series of draft resolutions were submitted by the Hon. J. Service, Premier and Colonial Treasurer of Victoria on the annexation of New Guinea, the New Hebrides, and other islands in the Western Pacific Ocean.

On 5 December 1883, the convention unanimously adopted a series of resolutions on the islands of the Pacific in the following form.

> 1. That further acquisition of dominion in the Pacific, south of the equator, by any foreign power would be highly detrimental to the safety and wellbeing of the British possessions in Australasia, and injurious to the interests of the empire.
>
> 2. That this convention refrains from suggesting the action by which effect can best be given to the foregoing resolution, in the confident belief that the Imperial Government will promptly adopt the wisest and most effectual measures for securing the safety and contentment of this portion of her Majesty's dominions.
>
> 3. That having regard to the geographical portion of the islands of New Guinea, the rapid extension of British trade and enterprise in Torres Strait, the certainty that the island will shortly be the resort of many adventurous subjects of Great Britain and other nations, and the absence or inadequacy of any existing laws for regulating their relations with the native tribes, this conference, while fully recognising that the responsibility of extending the boundaries of the empire belongs to the Imperial Government, is emphatically of opinion that such steps should be immediately taken as will most conveniently and effectively secure the incorporation with the British Empire of so much of New Guinea, and the small islands adjacent thereto as is not claimed by the Government of the Netherlands.
>
> 4. That, although the understanding arrived at in 1878 between

---
24 Hansard Commons Volume 283: 18 August 1883, Column 1117.

Great Britain and France recognising the independence of the New Hebrides, appears to preclude this convention from making any recommendation inconsistent with that understanding, the convention urges upon her Majesty's Government that it is extremely desirable that such understanding should give place to some more definite engagement, which shall secure these islands from falling under any foreign dominion; and at the same time the convention trusts that her Majesty's Government will avail itself of any opportunity that may arise for negotiating with the Government of France, with the object of obtaining the control of those islands in the interests of Australasia.

5. That the Governments represented at this convention undertake to submit and recommend to their respective Legislatures measures of permanent appropriation for defraying, in proportion to population, such share of the cost incurred in giving effect to the foregoing resolutions as her Majesty's Government, having regard to the relative importance of Imperial and Australasian interests, may seem fair and reasonable.

6. That the convention protests in the strongest manner against the declared intention of the Government of France to transport large numbers of relapsed criminals to the French possessions in the Pacific and urges her Majesty's Government to use every means in its power to prevent the adoption of a course so disastrous to the interest of Australasia and the Pacific islands.

7. That the convention expresses a confident hope that no penal settlement for the reception of European criminals will long continue to exist in the Pacific and invites her Majesty's Government to make to the Government of France such serious representations on this subject as may be deemed expedient.

8. That these resolutions be communicated to the Right Hon. the Secretary of State for the Colonies, together with a request that they may be submitted for her Majesty's gracious consideration, and for such action as her Majesty may think proper to direct, with a view to giving effect to the earnest desire of her loyal subjects in Australasia.

It was then decided that the resolutions should be forwarded at once to England, one copy to the Agents-General and one to the Earl of Derby, and they were despatched through Reuter's Telegraph Agency to England the same afternoon.[25]

---

25 Sydney Morning Herald 13 December 1883 p 11. Approved by Qld Parliament, Hansard

PROPOSED PROTECTORATE OVER NEW GUINEA.

The following despatch from Lord Derby to the Governors of the Australian Colonies:

> Downing-street,
>
> 9 May 1884.

2. I have explained in my despatch of July 11, 1883, to the Administrator of the Government of Queensland, which was before the convention, that in order to place Her Majesty's Government in a position to consider proposals for the protection or government of New Guinea or other places in the Western Pacific Ocean, it was desirable for the Australasian colonies to combine together effectively and provide the cost of carrying out any policy which it might be decided to adopt, and that in the meantime Her Majesty's Government must continue to decline proposals for large annexations of territory adjacent to Australia, adding that if a reasonable annual sum were provided by the colonies Her Majesty's Government would be prepared to strengthen the naval forces on the Australian station and make the High Commissionership more effective.

3. The convention does not appear to have taken this part of my despatch into consideration, but it agreed that the Governments represented at it should recommend their respective Legislatures to make permanent provision, in proportion to population, for the cost of the policy advocated, viz:

To check in whatever manner might be deemed wisest and most effectual the further acquisition of dominion in the Pacific south of the equator by any foreign power;

to secure the incorporation with the British empire of so much of New Guinea and the small islands adjacent thereto as is not claimed by the Government of the Netherlands; and

to acquire, if possible, the control of the New Hebrides in the interest of Australasia.

The Legislature of Queensland has recorded its entire concurrence in these resolutions, but no colony has taken measures to provide the requisite funds as suggested by the convention.

LA 26 February 1884 pp 475-478.

4. As, therefore, in the absence of any joint action by the colonies Her Majesty's Governments are not in a position to deal with those questions of policy to which I have referred, and some further delay seems unavoidable, it may be desirable that your Government should consider with the Governments of the other Australasian colonies whether there may not be an advantage in making provision for the intervening period in the manner suggested by me in paragraph 7 of my despatch of July 11 last, to Sir A. H. Palmer. As I then stated, her Majesty's Government are confident that no foreign power contemplates interference with New Guinea; but in the absence of any controlling authority, it is always possible that the subjects of a foreign power might require the protection or intervention of their Government, and British subjects also, by coming into collision with the natives or by setting up claims to land which would give much trouble hereafter.

5. Her Majesty's Government are disposed to think that there should be a High Commissioner, or at least, a deputy commissioner, with larger powers of independent action, stationed in or near the eastern coast of New Guinea, and that he should be furnished with a steamship independent of Her Majesty's naval squadron, and with a staff sufficient to enable him to exercise protection in the name of the Queen over these shores. The cost of this arrangement cannot be accurately estimated, as I have previously stated. But if one or more colonies will secure to Her Majesty's Government the payment of a sum of, say, £15,000 during the year ending 1 June 1885, they will be prepared to take immediate steps for establishing the High Commissioner's jurisdiction and will render to the contributing Governments an account of the expenditure incurred. It would be possible, after some months, to determine whether this arrangement should be further continued, and to consider fully with the colonial Governments (or with the Federal Council, if established) what arrangements should be made for the future supervision of the labour trade, if it should be decided that it can continue to be allowed. Her Majesty's Government have come to no conclusions as to the recommendations of the Western Pacific Committee, in regard to which the colonies should be first consulted; but I think it doubtful whether it will be found practicable to place the regulation of the labour traffic under Imperial control.

6. I may state, in conclusion, that the annual expenditure of this country in the maintenance of the squadron on the Australian station, including schooners and surveying vessels, is estimated as amounting at present to about £157,000.

I need hardly add that it is desirable that I should learn, as soon as possible, the result of the careful consideration which I trust that this despatch will receive from your government in conjunction with the Governments of the other Australasian colonies. (Signed) Derby.[26]

NEW GUINEA AND PACIFIC JURISDICTION CONTRIBUTION BILL.

On 24 July 1884, the Premier of Queensland said:

Mr. Speaker, this is a Bill to give effect to the promise made by the Government of this colony to contribute a portion of the £15,000 for the establishment of jurisdiction over the waters of New Guinea and the shores of that island.

As I have already stated, we have intimated to the colony of Victoria our willingness to join any of the other colonies, or Victoria alone, if necessary, in contributing the required amount. I understand, however, that all the colonies, except New Zealand, have now agreed to join in the guarantee. I think hon. members will agree that it is desirable, that action should be taken at once. I have therefore had a Bill framed, of which I sent a draft to Mr. Service, who is Chairman of the Permanent Committee, and I presume it has been circulated in the other colonies. Some suggestions have been made by him for its amendment by reciting the third and fourth resolutions agreed to by the Convention in the preamble, and other matters suggested by myself, and I believe we are now agreed as to the text of the Bill. The preamble recites the four resolutions which were adopted by the Convention bearing on the subject.

The Bill is very short. The first and principal clause is in the words of Lord Derby's despatch, which speaks of exercising protection, in the name of Her Majesty, over the eastern shores of New Guinea, and it provides that every year, while the Act is in force, there shall be paid to Her Majesty the stipulated amount. That exactly carries out the undertaking we gave, and the money is to be provided for the express purpose indicated in the despatch. As soon as the colonies pass a measure of this kind, there will be no longer any reason for any delay whatever in taking steps to establish protection over the shores of New Guinea. At present, we do not know to what extent that protection will be carried, but I am satisfied of this: that if Great

---

26 Daily Telegraph 27 June 1884 p 7.

Britain once exercises protection over the shores of New Guinea, it will not be very long before it is part of the British Empire.[27]

The New Guinea and Pacific Jurisdiction Contribution Act of 1884 — 48° VICTORIÆ, No. 7.

An Act to make provision for the Payment by the Colony of Queensland of a Proportionate Share of the Expenses to be incurred by Her Majesty's Government in giving effect to certain Resolutions adopted by the Convention of Representatives of the Governments of the several Australasian Colonies, held in Sydney in November and December, one thousand eight hundred and eighty-three. [Assented to 26 August 1884.][28]

AUSTRALIAN COLONIES — NEW GUINEA.

On 11 August 1884, in the Commons, Sir William MacArthur asked the Prime Minister whether the "Protection," mentioned in Lord Derby's Despatch of 9 May 1884, to the Governors of the Australian Colonies, as intended to be established in New Guinea will establish complete jurisdiction of the British Government over New Guinea and the adjacent Islands, so as to afford protection to the Natives, not only against the lawlessness of British subjects but against the lawlessness of the subjects of other Nations?

Mr. Gladstone replied:

> The protection mentioned in the Despatch of Lord Derby is in the nature of a protection which Her Majesty's Government advised the Queen to establish over so much of the coast of New Guinea as lies to the eastward of the Dutch Possessions but excluding some portions which lie to the North, as well as that portion which is claimed by Holland on the Northern side. I cannot, at this moment, give a minute definition now of the line up to which this Protectorate will extend; but within the limits of it, it will answer the purpose mentioned by my hon. Friend in his Question-that is to say, the jurisdiction of Her Majesty's Government will be sufficient to afford protection to the Natives against lawless action, by whomsoever taken, whether by

---

27 Hansard LA 24 July 1884 pp 165-167.
28 GG Supplement to the Queensland Government Gazette, 28 August 1884. No. 34, p 743.

British subjects or foreigners. The jurisdiction does not extend to the Islands to the North and East of New Guinea.[29]

On August 2, Count Hatzfeld of the German Foreign Office directed Count Munster, the German Ambassador in London, to bring to the attention of Lord Granville of the Foreign Office various points of difference between Berlin and London over affairs in the Pacific. Hatzfeld suggested that the despatches of July 11, 1883, and May 9, 1884, of Lord Derby, be used as the basis of negotiations.[30]

On 9 August 1884, Lord Granville of the Foreign Office wrote to Lord Ampthill, the British ambassador at Berlin, outlining the contents of a conversation he had with Count Münster:

> The German Ambassador called on me by appointment and informed me that his government wished to take steps to protect more efficiently those islands, and those parts of islands in the South Sea Archipelago, where German trade is largely developed and is daily increasing. Count Münster added that the wish of the Australian colonies to settle on the side of New Guinea opposite to Australia and to exclude from that part of the island settlements or establishments of other countries was regarded by the German Government as perfectly natural. But the German Government were of opinion that there are parts of the wild country on the north side of New Guinea which might be available as a field for German enterprise.
>
> With regard to New Guinea, on which island Germany had as yet founded no establishment, the German Government knew that communications had been taking place between the Home and Colonial Governments, and I might mention, but at present in confidence, that those communications are nearer a conclusion than is as yet known to the public.
>
> I added that the extension of some form of British authority in New Guinea, which will be shortly announced, will only embrace that part of the island which specially interests the Australian colonies, without prejudice to any territorial questions beyond those limits. Granville.[31]

---

29 House of Commons Hansard, 1884, Third Series, Volume 292, p 439.
30 Victoria Legislative Assembly, V. & P., 1885, III, # 36, pp. 39-40, Hatzfeld to Münster, August 2, 1884.
31 A. & P. 1884-5 c. 4273 p 4.

On 8 October 1884, the Colonial Office wrote to the Admiralty advising that Her Majesty's Government had decided that the establishment of the Queen's Protectorate and jurisdiction over the southern coast of New Guinea to the eastward of the 141st meridian of East longitude would be proclaimed, and requested the Admiralty to take the necessary steps for carrying the decision into execution and instruct the Commodore on the Australian Station by telegraph to proceed forthwith to New Guinea and proclaim Her Majesty's Protectorate as defined in this letter at a sufficient number of places along the coast:

> The Protectorate would for the present extend along the southern shore of New Guinea and over the country adjacent thereto, from the 141st meridian of East longitude before mentioned, eastward as far as East Cape, including any islands adjacent to the mainland in Goschen Strait, and to the southward of the said straits as far south and east as to include Kosmann Island. No persons will be permitted to settle or acquire land within the Protectorate unless expressly authorised by an officer of Her Majesty's Government.[32]

On 15 October 1884, Lord Derby advised the Governors of New South Wales, Victoria, Queensland, South Australia, Tasmania, Western Australia, and New Zealand that Her Majesty's Government had decided that the establishment of a protectorate over the southern coast of New Guinea and the adjacent islands would now be proclaimed and that the Admiralty had been requested to take the necessary steps for carrying the decision into execution.[33]

---

32 A. & P. 1884-85 c.4217 p 35.
33 A. & P. 1884-85 c.4217 p 40.

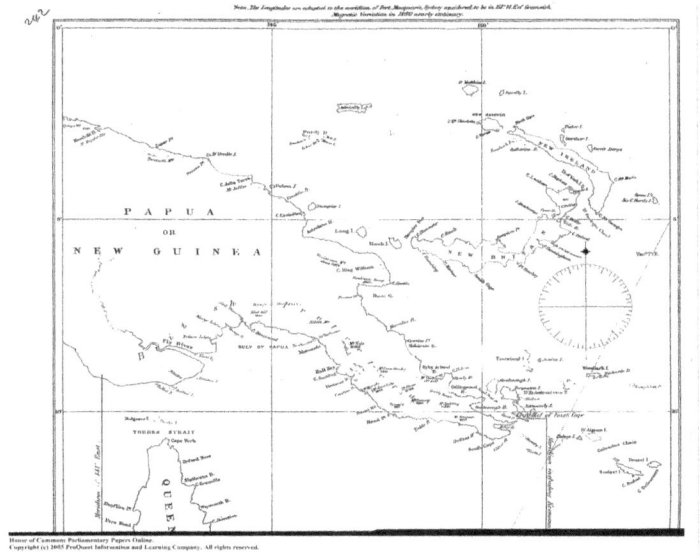

Admiralty chart showing the limits of the Protectorate of New Guinea, 22 October 1884.[34]

PROTECTORATE OF BRITISH NEW GUINEA.

Port Moresby, 6 November 1884. Commodore Erskine addressed the native chiefs, explaining to them the nature of the Protectorate, and enjoining them to respect the British flag, and to live peaceably and quietly under British rule. The Commodore then addressed Boi Vaga, Chief of the Motuan tribe, and presented him with a handsome massive stick with a silver head. The other native chiefs received presents, consisting of tomahawks, tobacco, calico, &c. Several heavy guns were fired, and the Gatlings and Nordenfeldts for the edification of the chiefs, who were greatly terrified.

> Now, I, James Elphinstone Erskine, Captain in the Royal Navy, and Commodore of the Australian station, one of Her Majesty's naval Aides-de-Camp, do hereby in the name of Her Most Gracious Majesty, declare and proclaim the establishment of such Protectorate over such portions of the coast and the adjacent islands as described in the schedule hereunto: all that portion of the southern shores of New Guinea, commencing from the boundary of that portion of

---

34 A. & P. 1884-85 c.4217 p 49.

the island claimed by the Government of the Netherlands, on the 141st meridian of East Longitude, to East Cape, with all the islands adjacent thereto, south of East Cape to Kosmann Island inclusive, together with islands in the Goschen Straits. Given at the Harbour of Port Moresby, on 6 November 1884. James Elphinstone Erskine, Commodore.[35]

When Commodore Erskine's above proclamation was published in the Queensland Government Gazette, the schedule to the proclamation was amended to include "and also the D'Entrecasteaux Group, and smaller islands adjacent".[36] Further to that, by a notice in the Queensland gazette of 24 December 1884, recruiting of Pacific Island Labourers was prohibited within the limits of the British Protectorate of New Guinea.[37]

GENERAL SCRATCHLEY'S INSTRUCTIONS.

On 19 November 1884, the Queensland government tabled in the Legislative Assembly correspondence regarding the appointment of Major-General Scratchley as Special Commissioner, and a request for further contributions from the Australasian colonies towards the maintenance of the Protectorate. By telegram, the Secretary of State for the Colonies dated 30 October advised as follows:

> Queen has approved of General Scratchley, Special Commissioner, to control protectorate in New Guinea. Will sail about 20 November. Her Majesty's Government think it desirable that colonies contributing to cost of protectorate shall appoint members of Council of Advice in Australia to assist him. Please inquire and state by telegraph whether your government and others contributing to Government agree to be represented in the Council. It is intended that Special Commissioner who will be independent of High Commissioner (Western Pacific) shall have jurisdiction over all persons within Protectorate and that no land shall be acquired there except through him. Also, will be Deputy Commissioner for portions of New Guinea outside Protectorate. Admiralty recommend purchase in England of steamer for Commissioner estimated cost

---

35 Brisbane Courier 15 November 1884 p 5.
36 GG VOL. XXXV.] 23 December 1884. [No. 113 p 2037. QSA ID ITM7169.
37 GG VOL. XXXV.] 24 December 1884. [No. 114 p 2040.

arrive in Sydney £16,000 or £18,000 to make him efficient. £15,000 guarantee must be apparently considerably increased. Telegraph whether contributing colonies will double their contributions for such purpose. If not, Scratchley must make best practicable arrangements he can after arrival in Australia.[38]

In response to the above request by Lord Derby, Mr. S. W. Griffith, Premier, advised that the Queensland government were willing to be represented on the proposed Council of Advice to assist the Special Commissioner for New Guinea, but desired to defer answering an additional contribution until they had further information as to the intention of her Majesty's Government relative to the New Guinea protectorate.[39]

Colonial Office, Downing Street,

17 November 1884

To Major General Scratchley, R.E., C.M.G.

Referring to my letter of this day's date respecting your duties as Special Commissioner in New Guinea, and as Deputy Commissioner under the Western Pacific Orders-in-Council, I am directed by Earl Derby to inform you that the salary of the combined appointment has been fixed at £2500 a year to be defrayed from money's provided by the colonies. Mr. Romilly is now in receipt of £300 a year from Imperial funds as Deputy Commissioner, and you are authorised to pay him a further £200 a year so long as he continues to serve in the protectorate. You are further at liberty to pay your private secretary at the rate of £300 a year from the same source. It will be essential that you should keep careful and accurate accounts of your financial transactions and submit them for audit, as shall hereafter be directed. R G W. Herbert.

On 17 November 1884, Lord Derby also wrote to Sir G. W. Des Voeux, acting High Commissioner for the Western Pacific confirming Major-General Peter Henry Scratchley, R.E., C.M.G., appointment as Deputy Commissioner for the Western Pacific for the district north of latitude 15° south, and to the west of longitude 160° east, and for so much of the Solomon Islands as lies beyond those limits. Derby further advised that a protectorate would be

---

38 Brisbane Courier 20 November 1884 p 5.
39 Brisbane Courier 20 November 1884 p 5.

established over a portion of New Guinea and that Major-General Scratchley was to be Special Commissioner for that Protectorate. Derby also observed that the territory comprised in the Protectorate would continue to be within the operation of the Western Pacific Orders in Council; and that he should possess the powers of a Deputy Commissioner. Therefore, Derby proposed to instruct him to act upon his discretion in matters arising under the Western Pacific Orders in Council but to inform Des Voeux of any action which he may take, and of which it was proper that Des Voeux should be informed.[40]

Sir Peter Scratchley, R.C.M.C. (1885). Melbourne: Alfred Martin Ebsworth.

The Special Commissioner for the protected territory in New Guinea, through the office of the Colonial Secretary's Office, Brisbane, on 19 February 1885 published, for general information, instructions issued in connection with the administration of New

---

40 A. & P. 1884-85 C.4273 p 32.

Guinea in the Queensland government gazette of 21 February 1885.[41] On 2 October 1885, the Special Commissioner published updated instructions in connection with the administration of New Guinea in the Queensland government gazette, among others, as follows:

> Portions of coast unsafe to Traders and others.
>
> Traders and others are cautioned against visiting the following portions of the coast and islands in the Protectorate: From Kerepunu to South Cape (including Moresby Island), D'Entrecasteaux Group, Engineer Group, Woodlark Group, Jurien and Jouvency islands; also, from East Cape to the German boundary on the northeast coast.[42]

THE ABORIGINES OF NEW GUINEA

Shortly before his departure, a deputation of the Aborigines Protection Society waited upon General Scratchley to congratulate him upon his appointment and enlist his assistance in suppressing the kidnapping of the natives of New Guinea, already commenced in the interests of sugar planters. Mr. F. W. Chesson pointed out that the Rev. Mr. Chalmers had recently complained to Baron Miklouho Maclay, who had brought the fact under the society's notice that the part of the coast where he especially laboured had been visited by labour vessels that had kidnapped recruits. Evidence was forthcoming in support of these allegations, which might not only bring the perpetrators of the outrage to justice but also lead to the return of the kidnapped natives to their homes. Sir W. M'Arthur, M.P., and several other gentlemen having expressed themselves in support of Mr. Chesson, General Scratchley replied, thanking the society for their encouragement and sympathy. He did not, he said, underestimate the difficulties that awaited him, but for the present, they would be reduced by the country being closed to white settlement. When it was thrown open, of course, the difficulties would increase very largely but it was useless to anticipate. From

---

41   GG VOL. XXXVI.] 21 February 1885. [No. 33 p 557.
42   GG VOL. XXXVII.] 2 October 1885. [No. 59 p 1163.

his long connexion with Australia, he was fully satisfied that the colonists held the same opinions and had the same aspirations as the English at home. There might be a great number of individual cases where cruelty had been committed, but he thought that due consideration should be given to the surrounding circumstances. As to New Guinea, he did not believe, except for Queensland, that there could be any desire to procure labour from that island. In the first place, the islanders were not considered to be particularly good for labour purposes. He felt that he would be supported by the Australian Governments in any steps he might consider necessary to take for the protection of the natives. That was, after all, the primary object of appointing him. Sir William M'Arthur thanked General Scratchley, and the deputation withdrew.[43]

THE GERMANS IN NEW GUINEA

Herr Greiner of the German Consulate-General at Sydney, on 18 November 1884, reported the establishment of an English protectorate over the south coast of New Guinea, of November 8, and forwarded a copy of Commodore Erskine's proclamation to Prince Bismarck.[44]

The officer commanding the German man-of-war *Elisabeth* at Cooktown, on December 17, 1884, advised the German home government by telegraph that "our men-of-war have hoisted the German flag at several points on the north coast of New Guinea, east of the Dutch boundary, and in New Britain, to protect those purchases of land by German subjects backed (understützt) by treaties made with native chiefs".[45]

Melbourne, December 31. The Premier of Victoria sent the following telegram to the Agent-General:

> All the colonies deplore the inaction which has resulted in the present fiasco as regards New Guinea, but some of them differ as

---

43 Argus 27 December 1884 p 5.
44 VParl, 1885 GERMAN INTERESTS IN THE SOUTH SEA, No. 35, p 44.
45 VParl, 1885 GERMAN INTERESTS IN THE SOUTH SEA, No. 36, p 44.

to the best mode of expressing their dissatisfaction, and each will communicate with its own Agent-General. Queensland has already done so. Protest emphatically on behalf of Victoria and Tasmania against the recognition of German claims in New Guinea. The state of facts forces us to one or the other of the following conclusions: either Lord Derby has been deceived, or he has deceived us. His supineness or neglect is simply lamentable. If New Guinea be not reclaimed and the New Hebrides preserved, the feeling of estrangement will indubitably increase. We feel very bitterly on the subject. A copy of this message was telegraphed to the Premiers of the other colonies.[46]

On 19 June 1885, the following notice appeared in the *London Gazette* setting out the agreement between the Governments of Great Britain and Germany as to the boundaries of the possessions of the two countries in New Guinea:

> Downing-street, June 18, 1885.
>
> The point on the north-east coast of New Guinea where the 8th parallel of south latitude cuts the coast forms the boundary on the coast, and a line described as under, determines the boundaries inland of the respective territories: Starting from the coast in the neighbourhood of Mitre Rock on the 8th parallel of south latitude and following this parallel to the point where it is cut by the 147th degree of east longitude, then in a straight line in a north-westerly direction to the point where the 6th parallel of south latitude cuts the 144th degree of east longitude and continuing in a west-north-westerly direction to the point of intersection of the 5th parallel of south latitude and the 141st degree of east longitude.
>
> The British Possessions lie to the south of the line, thus defined, the German to the north. The British Possessions will not include Long Island, nor Hook Island, nor any islands adjacent to New Guinea to the northward of the 8th parallel of south latitude.[47]

Berlin, May 21, 1885. Emperor William granted a charter to the German New Guinea Company, whose territory he named, Kaiser Wilhelm's Land, which also included the adjacent islands of the Bismarck Archipelago; this charter established a State and judicial

---

46 Brisbane Courier 1 January 1885 pp 5 & 6.
47 VPARL 1885 No. 35 p 15. GG Vol. XXXVII.] 15 August 1885. [No. 28, p 621.

system subject to the supremacy of Germany.[48]

Colonial Secretary's Office, Brisbane,

6 August 1885.

His Excellency the Governor has been pleased to direct the publication, for general information, of the following translation of a Proclamation issued by the Imperial Commissioner for the German Protectorate of New Guinea.

For and on behalf of the German Protectorate on the Continent of New Guinea, "Kaiser Wilhelm's Land," and for and on behalf of the Islands of the Bismarck Archipelago, "formerly known as the Archipelago of New Britain," I, in pursuance of instructions received, do hereby notify as follows, viz.:

1. Fresh acquisitions of territory, without the sanction of the German authorities, are invalid, and only old and well-established rights will be acknowledged.

2. Arms, Ammunition, and Explosives, as also Spirituous Liquors, are, in the meantime, not allowed to be given to Aborigines.

3. It is hereby expressly prohibited to carry away Aborigines from off the German Protectorate for the purpose of being employed as Labourers, except it be for German Plantations, and from those portions of the Archipelago of New Britain where this practice has obtained hitherto, and then only under the supervision of German (Government) Officials.

The Imperial Commissioner for the German Protectorate. (Signed) VON OERTZEN.[49]

DEATH OF SIR PETER SCRATCHLEY

Townsville, December 3. Sir Peter Scratchley was first seized with malarial fever whilst cruising off Bentley Bay, on the north-east coast of New Guinea, on 21 November. The steamer arrived at Cooktown on 30 November. The patient was seen by Dr. Kortüm. The *Governor Blackall* left that evening at full speed for Townsville.

---

48 Brisbane Courier 23 May 1885 p 5.
49 GG Vol. XXXVII.] 8 August 1885 [No. 24 p 582. Brisbane Courier 3 February 1886 p 6 German Colonial Policy.

While coming down the coast the patient gradually got weaker, and at 1 a.m. on 2 December 1885, died.[50]

The *Brisbane Courier,* in an editorial of 4 December 1885, observed:

> Every circumstance connected with the acquisition and occupation of New Guinea has been unfortunate, but it would be the greatest misfortune that has yet befallen English interests in the Pacific if Sir Peter Scratchley's successor should be one of Sir Arthur Gordon's underlings. That officer had great influence with the English Government through his family connections and his assiduous cultivation of the Exeter Hall party, but no English Governor was ever so thoroughly detested by all white men, and Englishmen especially, on this side of the globe, and his subordinates trained in his school would be no better liked. We ask why should not an Australian be chosen for this post. We can see no reason why the Hon. John Douglas should not receive, by an appointment to a post for which he is peculiarly fitted under the Imperial Government, recognition of the services which in many capacities both as a private individual and as a public man he has during the past thirty years rendered to this colony.[51]

JOHN DOUGLAS — NEW GUINEA SPECIAL COMMISSIONER

On 9 January 1886, the hon. Frederick Stanley, Secretary for the Colonies advised Sir A. Musgrave, Governor of the appointment of Mr. John Douglas as Special Commissioner in New Guinea, and creating him a Deputy Commissioner of the Western Pacific as follows:

> Downing Street,
>
> 20 January 1886
>
> John Douglas, Esq, I had the honour to enclose in my despatch general of the 8th instant a commission as Special Commissioner over the whole of British New Guinea and the adjacent islands. As

---

50 Brisbane Courier 4 December 1885 p 5 & 8 December 1885 p 5 The Late Sir Peter Scratchley.
51 Brisbane Courier 4 December 1885 p 4.

you are aware, the protectorate has been largely added to since the late Sir Peter Scratchley's first commission was issued.

2. Sir Peter Scratchley's despatches showed that he did not fully understand that, unless the territory included in the protectorate becomes British soil by the declaration of Her Majesty's sovereignty over it, the Queen does not possess and therefore could not delegate to him a general power to make laws which will bind persons other than her own subjects. As regards the latter she may, as you probably are aware, by Order-in-Council under the Foreign Jurisdiction Acts, establish courts, and make such other regulations as she thinks necessary for their control.

3. This power she has exercised in respect to the South Seas by means of the Western Pacific Orders-in-Council, and as those orders extend to New Guinea and the adjacent islands, it was considered unnecessary to issue a fresh order specially affecting the protectorate.

4. I have caused a similar commission to be issued to you, and you will thus possess civil and criminal jurisdiction over British subjects; but the orders do not extend to foreigners, over whom you will have no judicial authority, except in such civil matters as they may wish to bring before you. Special provision for their doing so is made by section 145 of the Western Pacific Order-in-Council of 1877.

5. In addition to this judicial authority, your commission, as special commissioner, empowers you in all respects to represent the Queen's authority and to do all such things as, in the interest of her service, you may think expedient. You are therefore at liberty to make such regulations as you think necessary, compliance with which may be made a condition of residence in the Protectorate if you are able to enforce them. Fred. A. Stanley.[52]

THE FUTURE ADMINISTRATION OF BRITISH NEW GUINEA

The future government of New Guinea was made the subject of a very able and exhaustive memorandum by Mr. Griffith, which was drawn up after consultation with the Hon. John Douglas, High

---

52   Brisbane Courier 20 March 1886 p 4-5 & 24 March 1886 p 2. GG VOL. XXXVIII.] 22 March 1886. [No. 38 p 1105.

Commissioner for the Protectorate. The plan broadly proposed that the Imperial Government would proclaim sovereignty over the protectorate, thus securing for the administrator some legal powers of which he possessed virtually none as presently constituted, and would make some contribution, by way of gift or loan to the establishment of a government. The Queensland government would be responsible for an annual subsidy of £15,000 per annum taking pro rata contributions from such colonies as were willing to make them. The future government of New Guinea was to be carried on by an Administrator assisted by a local council, who were to be under the general control of the Governor of Queensland, and he, in turn, was to take the advice of his Executive Council in dealing with New Guinea matters. The annual budget was to be submitted by the Administrator to the Governor and approved before being submitted to a local council. The contributing colonies were to be informed of all that was done in New Guinea but were not to be consulted except in extraordinary and special cases. Speaking generally, the scheme provided for the future New Guinea Administration to be supervised, not by the Queensland Parliament, but by the Governor, aided by the advice of Ministers responsible to the Queensland Parliament. The memorandum was sent as a circular to the Governments of the Australian colonies, and the Press references to it in the principal Southern newspapers were favourable.[53]

MEMORANDUM ON NEW GUINEA.

On 20 May 1886, Mr. S. Griffith wrote to the Administrator of the government of Queensland advising that he had addressed a letter, dated 30 March 1886, to the governments of the other Australian colonies enclosing a copy of his Memorandum. The Government of South Australia replied on 5 April declining to be a party to the cost of the government of New Guinea.

Draft Proposals for the future Administration of British New

---

53 Brisbane Courier 21 Apr 1886 p 3. Brisbane Courier 2 April 1886 pp 4-5.

Guinea agreed to by the governments of the colonies of New South Wales, Queensland, and Victoria, at Sydney, on 28 April 1886:

Memorandum agreed to:

I. The colony of Queensland to undertake by a permanent Appropriation Act to defray the cost of the administration of the Government of British New Guinea to an extent not exceeding £15,000 per annum for the term of five years, subject to the following conditions:

II. The colonies of New South Wales and Victoria to undertake by similar permanent Appropriation Acts to bear equally with Queensland any amount which the latter colony may be called upon to pay under article I so that each colony shall be liable for one-third of the whole expenditure to an extent not exceeding £5000.

III. Any contribution made by the Governments of any of the other Australasian colonies to be applied in reduction of the amount which the colonies may be called upon to pay under articles I. and II.

IV. Any revenue raised by the Government of New Guinea to be similarly applied in reduction of the amount which the colonies may be called upon to pay under articles I and II, unless in the event of a larger annual expenditure than £15,000 being agreed to, as provided in article XVI., in which case the excess is to be provided from the revenue.

V. The Imperial Government to make a reasonable contribution (by way of loan or otherwise) towards the cost of efficiently starting the Government, and the necessary government buildings, etc.

VI. Upon the proposed guarantee being given by Queensland, her Majesty to assume sovereignty over the protectorate.

VII. An Administrator of the Government to be appointed with that title, to whom, with two or more other persons, legislative powers are to be delegated under the Imperial Acts 6 and 7 Victoria c. 13 and 23, and 24 Victoria c. 121.

VIII. The colonies, recognising the necessity for a small civil list, propose the following as probably sufficient for the first initiation of the Government:

Administrator £1,500

Private Secretary £300

Judicial Officer £1,000

Secretary to Government £500

IX. No purchase of land to be allowed to be made by private persons except from the Government or purchasers from it.

X. No deportation of natives to be allowed either from one part of the colony to another or to places beyond the colony, except under ordinances reserved for her Majesty's assent and assented to by her Majesty.

XI. Trading with the natives in arms, ammunition, explosives, and intoxicants to be prohibited except under ordinances reserved and assented to in like manner.

XII. No differential duties to be imposed in favour of any of the guaranteeing colonies, or any other colony or country.

XIII. The foregoing four articles to be made part of the Constitution of the colony, preferably by Orders-in-Council made contemporaneously with the assumption of sovereignty, or else by ordinances to be passed immediately afterwards under instructions to the Administrator from her Majesty's Imperial Government. Standing instructions to be given to the Governor of Queensland and to the Administrator of British New Guinea to observe the conditions of these articles.

XIV. An appeal to lie to the Supreme Court of Queensland, at Brisbane, in all civil cases involving an amount of over £100, and in all criminal cases involving a punishment greater than three months imprisonment.

XV. An estimate of revenue and expenditure to be submitted by the Administrator to the Governor of Queensland and approved by him before the passing of any appropriation ordinance. The Governor of Queensland to have power to disallow any item of proposed expenditure.

XVI. Any appropriation beyond the amount of £15,000 for any one year to be agreed to by each of the three guaranteeing colonies.

XVII All accounts of receipts and expenditure to be audited by officers of the Queensland Government.

XVIII. The Administrator, in the exercise of his legislative and administrative functions, to be subject to the instructions of the Governor of Queensland (subject of course to her Majesty's power of disallowance of proposed laws).

XIX. The Governor of Queensland to be directed to consult his Executive Council upon all matters relating to British New Guinea.

XX. The Government of Queensland to consult the Governments of the other contributing colonies in all matters other than those of ordinary administration, and to report to them all action taken.

XXI. An annual report to be furnished by the Administrator to the Governor of Queensland of the proceedings of the Government (legislative and administrative), and copies of such report together with any observations which the Governor of Queensland may think fit to make thereon, to be forwarded to the Secretary of State and to each of the contributing colonies

4. If her Majesty should be pleased to approve of these proposals, this Government will be prepared at once to ask the legislature to pass the necessary Act for the permanent appropriation of the agreed sum of £15,000 without waiting for any similar Acts to be passed by the Legislatures of New South Wales and Victoria.

5. This Government wishes, however, that it should be stipulated as between her Majesty's Government and the colony of Queensland that if from any cause the agreed contribution should not be paid by New South Wales or Victoria, Queensland should have a first charge upon any surplus revenue of British New Guinea for any amount which she is called upon to pay under her guarantee beyond the agreed proportion of one-third.

6. Your Excellency will observe that the term for which it is proposed that the guarantee should be given is five years. This term was agreed upon after full discussion I do not think that the other colonies would be disposed to join in a longer guarantee, and they prefer that the guarantee to be now given by Queensland should be for the same term for which they are willing to contribute. I have no doubt that before the expiration of that period, many of the uncertainties now surrounding the matter will be removed, and that there will be no difficulty in entering into such fresh arrangements as circumstances may then show to be most expedient.

7. With respect to the proposed initial contribution from the Imperial Government, no fixed amount has been asked for. Nor is it likely that a very large amount would be required immediately. It would, however, be necessary to provide buildings of various

kinds in different places and probably also, during the five years to purchase a steamer and other vessels or boats. It has been suggested that a contribution should be made of the same amount as was made in the case of Fiji—£100,000.

8. I have now the honour to request your Excellency to be good enough to communicate these proposals to the Secretary of State for her Majesty's consideration, and I venture to express the hope that they may lead to an early settlement of the question. S. W. Griffith.[54]

OPENING OF QUEENSLAND PARLIAMENT.

The fourth session of the Ninth Parliament of Queensland was opened by his Excellency the Administrator (Sir Arthur Palmer) on 13 July 1886. In respect of the future administration of the government of British New Guinea, Sir Arthur Palmer said the matter was still unsettled; that his Ministers had formulated proposals on the subject, which had received the assent of the governments of the colonies of New South Wales and Victoria, and under which the primary responsibility of the administration would devolve upon Queensland. He added that he was confident that these proposals would meet with members' concurrence, and he would be able to inform members that they had received her Majesty's approval and to recommend the necessary measures to give effect to them.[55]

In November 1886, Sir S. W. Griffith made a statement in the House. "The correspondence laid on the table of the House this session had brought the matter down to its latest development so far as formal communications between the Queensland government, the governments of the other colonies, and the Imperial Government, were concerned. The letter that he had addressed to the Administrator of the Government on 20 May last embodied the terms of a scheme or proposals for the future administration of New Guinea, which was agreed to by the Governments of New

---

54 Hansard LA, 24 November 1886 pp 1842-1846. Brisbane Courier 22 May 1886 p 5.
55 Brisbane Courier 14 July 1886 p 5.

South Wales, Queensland, and Victoria at a meeting held between Mr. Gillies, Sir Patrick Jennings, and himself on 28 April. New Zealand and Tasmania had formally agreed to the proposals, but South Australia, as they knew, had withdrawn formally from any further participation in the matter. Western Australia and Fiji being Crown colonies would have to wait instructions from the Imperial Government. Their contributions were, however, very small, and the more practical colonies were agreed in the matter which imposed no undue burden upon anybody. This scheme contemplated the government of British New Guinea being to a certain extent under the control of the government of Queensland."

Brisbane, 6 December 1886. The Administrator of the government received an important cable message from the Hon. E. S. Stanhope, Secretary of State for the Colonies, to the following effect:

> Her Majesty's Government have very carefully considered the correspondence regarding New Guinea. I desire to state frankly their opinion on the colonial proposals for establishing a sovereignty over British New Guinea involves the possibility of very heavy expenditure with prospects of small revenue and is not necessary to the defence of Australia from foreign aggression, that object being adequately secured by a protectorate. A sovereignty might be proclaimed at certain limited spots, as at the Gold Coast, but £15,000 per annum would be insufficient for even those arrangements. A sovereignty as at the Gold Coast and Lagos would involve an expenditure of £150,000 a year and more. Annexation and settlement are of no advantage to this country, and we doubt whether any advantage would accrue to the Australian colonies commensurate with the cost to them. If, however, annexation and settlement is still desired in lieu of the present proposals, a financial arrangement in accordance with them would have to be reconsidered. The present proposals contemplate a small colonial contribution for five years, this country being responsible for ultimate and future charges. We could not proceed except on the converse principle, viz., this country giving a small initial contribution, as offered in August 1885, and the colonies securing a sufficient annual sum by a permanent act, not limited to five years. Many points in Mr. Griffiths' proposals are good, but we cannot consider the details of them until the financial difficulties are removed.[56]

---

56 Age 7 December 1886 p 6. Brisbane Courier 9 December 1886 p 5.

Brisbane, 21 December 1886. The Governor received a further cablegram from the Right Hon. E. Stanhope about the telegraphic despatch on New Guinea of 6 December, to the following effect:

> What is desired (in that despatch) is simply to make clear that her Majesty's Government do not see any prospect of £15,000 per annum being sufficient, or how they could proclaim sovereignty with the probability of its subsequent withdrawal. Investors and natives must have security against abandonment of the country after it is once occupied, and Great Britain cannot undertake any unknown cost.[57]

On 13 October 1887, in introducing the British New Guinea (Queensland) Bill of 1887, the Premier said that in April 1886 certain proposals had been agreed to by the governments of the three colonies of Queensland, New South Wales, and Victoria for the future administration of British New Guinea.[58] Those proposals had been communicated to the Imperial Government, and the matter then remained in abeyance until the Conference in London of last April 1887. At that time, the Imperial Government was willing to accept the proposals with practically only one modification, and that was that Queensland should guarantee, on behalf of the other colonies, that the £15,000 should be paid for ten years instead of five, as provided in the draft proposals. There was another modification, which consisted in the Imperial Government defining exactly what their contribution to the initial expenses of the government of New Guinea would be. He did not think he need refer to it in detail. Other than reciting the original proposals of the three Governments in the first schedule (the Memorandum above); then reciting that those proposals were agreed to by the Imperial Government with certain modifications and setting out the amended proposals in the second schedule of the Bill; and then reciting that the amended proposals were agreed to by the representatives of the governments of the Australasian colonies.[59]

---

57 Brisbane Courier 21 December 1886 p 4.
58 See pp 56-59 above, Memorandum agreed to by Qld, NSW & Vic.
59 Hansard LA 13 October 1887 pp 1043-1045.

THE SECOND SCHEDULE.

Amended Proposals by the Imperial Government for the Administration of British New Guinea.

1. The Colony of Queensland to undertake by a special Act to defray the cost of the administration of the Government of British New Guinea to an extent not exceeding £15,000 per annum for the term of ten years, subject to the following conditions:

2. The Colonies of New South Wales and Victoria to undertake by similar Acts to bear equally with Queensland any amount which the latter Colony may be called upon to pay under Article 1 so that each Colony shall be liable for one-third of the whole expenditure to an extent not exceeding £5,000.

3. Any contribution made by the Governments of any of the other Australasian Colonies to be applied in reduction of the amount which the Colonies may be called upon to pay under Articles 1 and 2.

4. Any revenue raised by the Government of New Guinea to be similarly applied in reduction of the amount which the Colonies may be called upon to pay under Articles. 1 and 2, unless in the event of a larger annual expenditure than £15,000 being agreed to, as provided in Article 16, in which case the excess is to be provided from the revenue.

5. Her Majesty's Imperial Government to contribute a suitable steam vessel for the service of the Territory, at a cost not exceeding £18,500, with the cost of its maintenance during the first three years estimated at about £3,500 a year.

6. Upon the passing of the above-mentioned Special Act, Her Majesty to assume Sovereignty over the Protectorate.

7. An Administrator of the Government to be appointed, to whom, with two or more other persons, legislative powers are to be delegated by Letters Patent under the Imperial Acts 6 and 7 Vic. cap. 13, and 23 and 24 Vic. cap. 121.

8. The following sums to be reserved in the Letters Patent by way of Civil List:

Administrator £1,500

Private Secretary 300

Judicial Officer 1,000

Secretary to Government 500

9. No purchase of land to be allowed to be made by private persons, except from the Government or purchasers from it.

10. No deportation of natives to be allowed either from one part of the Territory to another or to places beyond the Territory, except under Ordinances reserved for Her Majesty's assent and assented to by Her Majesty.

11. Trading with the natives in arms, ammunition, explosives, and intoxicants to be prohibited, except under Ordinances reserved and assented to in like manner.

12. No differential duties to be imposed in favour of any of the Guaranteeing Colonies, or any other colony or country.

13. The foregoing four Articles to be embodied in the Letters Patent as part of the constitution of the Territory.

14. An appeal to lie to the Supreme Court of Queensland, at Brisbane, in all civil cases involving an amount of over £100, and in all criminal cases involving a punishment greater than three months imprisonment. The necessary legislation for this purpose to be passed to the Imperial and Queensland Parliaments.

15. An estimate of revenue and expenditure to be submitted by the Administrator to the Governor of Queensland and approved by him before the passing of any Appropriation Ordinance. The Governor of Queensland to have power to disallow any item of proposed expenditure.

16. Any appropriation beyond the amount of £15,000 for any one year to be agreed to by each of the three guaranteeing colonies.

17. All accounts of receipts and expenditure to be audited by officers of the Queensland Government.

18. The Administrator, in the exercise of his legislative and administrative functions, to be guided by the instructions of the Governor of Queensland (subject to Her Majesty's power of disallowance of proposed laws).

19. The Governor of Queensland to be directed to consult his Executive Council upon all matters relating to British New Guinea.

20. The Government of Queensland to consult the Governments of the other contributing colonies in all matters other than those of ordinary administration, and to report to them all action taken.

21. The Administrator to be instructed to furnish to the Governor of Queensland an annual report of the proceedings of the Government (Legislative and Administrative), and copies of such report, together with any observations which the Governor of Queensland may think fit to make thereon, to be forwarded to the Secretary of State, and to each of the contributing Colonies.

MEMORANDUM

It is understood that Queensland is to have a first charge upon any surplus revenue of British New Guinea for any amount which the Colony may be called upon to pay under the Special Act beyond the agreed.

NEW GUINEA — PROCLAMATION OF BRITISH SOVEREIGNTY

The following despatch and enclosure descriptive of the ceremonies attending the proclamation of British sovereignty over a portion of New Guinea were received by Sir Anthony Musgrave.

Government House, Granville,

Port Moresby,

5 September 1888.

Governor of Queensland.

I left Cooktown in *HMS Opal* on the 1st instant and arrived here on the 4th.

2. At 4 o'clock of the afternoon of the same day there were assembled at Government House, Captain Bosanquet, with the officers and men of *HMS Opal*, the officers of the Protectorate, and the European residents of the place, and about 200 natives of whom the larger

number belonged to the Port Moresby district. In the presence of these, I read a proclamation declaring the protected territory to be from that time a British possession. I then read the letters patent, at the conclusion of which I briefly drew the attention of the audience to the importance of the event and directed the royal standard to be hoisted, which was saluted by *HMS Opal* with twenty-one guns. I then read my commission, and took from Captain Bosanquet, as the senior officer there present in the Queen's service, the oath of allegiance and the oath of office as Administrator.

3. A detailed note of the proceedings, taken by Mr. Musgrave, is enclosed herewith.

4. I enclose a copy of the proclamation, signed, and sealed. Copies of the first *Government Gazette*, containing the proclamation, the letters patent, and my own commission as Administrator, will go by next mail.

I have forwarded a duplicate of this despatch, with its contents, to the Right Hon. the Secretary of State for the Colonies. Wm. Macgregor. Administrator New Guinea.[60]

THE MACHINERY OF ANNEXATION AND GOVERNMENT OF BRITISH NEW GUINEA — BRITISH NEW GUINEA ACT OF 1887 (QUEENSLAND).

Whereas divers of Our subjects have heretofore resorted to and settled in divers places within the Territory and Islands hereunder described, in which there is no civilised Government.

And whereas the said Territory and Islands will not have been acquired by cession or conquest, and will not be within the jurisdiction of the Legislature of any British Possession.

And whereas We are minded, as and when the said Territory and Islands shall become part of Our Dominions, to erect the same into a separate Possession, and to provide for the Government thereof.

---

60 Brisbane Courier 20 September 1888 p 7. GG VOL. XLV.] 2 October 1888. [No. 27, p 405. GG VOL. XLV.] 11 September 1888. [No. 9, pp 121-133.

Now therefore We constitute, and erect the said Territory and Islands as above described into a separate Possession and Government by the name of British New Guinea.

18. The Administrator, in the exercise of his legislative and administrative functions, to be guided by the instructions of the Governor of Queensland (subject to Her Majesty's power of disallowance of proposed laws).

19. The Governor of Queensland to be directed to consult his Executive Council upon all matters relating to British New Guinea.

20. The Government of Queensland to consult the Governments of the other contributing Colonies in all matters other than those of ordinary administration, and to report to them all action taken.

21. The Administrator to be instructed to furnish to the Government of Queensland an annual report of the proceedings of the Government (Legislative and Administrative), and copies of such report, together with any observation which the Governor of Queensland may think fit to make thereon, to be forwarded to the Secretary of State, and to each of the contributing Colonies.

2

ASSESSMENT

This book is about marine incidents that occurred from 1859 to Federation regarding Queensland's participation in the exploration, conversion, exploitation, possession, and governance of a group of people described as Papuan within the territory formerly known as British New Guinea.

Therefore, I will not be covering all the marine incidents that occurred during the colonial period of contact with the colony of British New Guinea. The marine incidents portrayed in this narrative have an element of indigenous participation. The indigenous element is the native-born Melanesian peoples of Papua, New Guinea. The identified marine incidents, the subject of this book, are set out below at pages 114 to 116.

The question is how and in what way did indigenous elements cross or intersect the maritime jurisdiction, who were these indigenous elements and what was the manner and method (form) of this interaction as to time, place, or other circumstances attending the incident; what was the manner and evidence of the indigenous contact?

I now come to the most challenging and complex part of the project, and that is to offer an assessment of the contact between outsiders and the indigenous inhabitants of New Guinea. I suppose the simplest approach is to tell it how it was. The problem then is, by which yardstick do I tell the tale?

Here is a good example of the many challenging aspects associated with telling the tale. The *Brisbane Courier* of 10 December 1878 reported on New Guinea as follows:

> A country with boundless capabilities of soil and climate for tropical products, peopled by a kindly, industrious, and most interesting race-not the ruthless savages pictured by fancy, but living in villages, engaging in rude arts and manufactures, observing good faith, and acknowledging the obligations of hospitality towards their white visitors.[61]

A group of white people who were living and working in New Guinea in 1878 disputed this benign portrayal of the natives:

> On November 5, two aged and helpless women belonging to a bush tribe in the vicinity of Kerepunu entered the village adjoining our bêche-de-mer stations for trading. For some reason, they were seized and brutally murdered, and their bodies thrown into the water. This, as an instance of their savage spirit, is nothing compared with the horrible act that took place some few days before. The Kara natives in battle with a bush tribe made four prisoners, whom they bound hand and foot and carried to their village. Here the prisoners were thrown, bound like sheep, on the ground, while their captors built a large fire. They then proceeded to cut them up alive, inch by inch, commencing at the joints of their fingers, then their toes, until nothing was left of the unfortunate creatures but their still living trunks; their heads were then cut off, and the skulls boiled. These are by no means rare instances, as Captain Webb, of the *Pride of the Logan*, was often obliged, during his stay on this part of the coast, to be a witness to similar scenes. They are also the most inveterate thieves, as Mr. Ingham can testify, and of very treacherous disposition, as they have several times attacked us without provocation while pretending to be friendly. This may open the eyes of many admirers of the New Guinea natives to their real merits and virtues. The tale we have quoted sufficiently establishes the hideous nature of the cannibal savage.[62]

---

61 Brisbane Courier 10 December 1878 p 2.
62 Brisbane Courier 14 December 1878 p 5.

Mr. Musgrave, an Assistant Deputy Commissioner, after compiling a list of attacks, massacres, and outrages on foreigners by British New Guinea natives formed the view that the Papuan native was inclined to be treacherous, bloodthirsty, and greedy for plunder. Musgrave added, "he (the native) was, however, wonderfully cunning in disguising these feelings, and even amongst the most experienced white men succeeded in inspiring dangerously unguarded confidence".[63]

The Hon. Dr. Macgregor, who represented the Crown colony of Fiji at the time, made a speech at the Federal Council, at Hobart in February 1886, which may offer an approach to analysing first contact incidents with indigenous elements:

> I can only express the strongest disapprobation of expeditions of that kind being sent to New Guinea. We are all very anxious and curious to know what is: the source of the rivers, the height of the mountains, and the natural products of New Guinea. But, in my opinion, such expeditions are liable to do a great deal more harm than all the good they can accomplish. Those engaged in them proceed to New Guinea without knowing where they are going or what they are going for. They go for anything and everything they can lay their hands on. They have no idea in whose country they are or on whose land they are going, and I know very well from experience that white men going to the country of black men are very apt to be impressed with the idea that anything they come across is everybody's property. I also know very well, from experience, that in most islands in the Pacific, it will be somewhat difficult to find a piece of land that has not got an owner. In many islands, I doubt whether it was possible to find a fruit tree that has not got its owner. These private expeditions proceed into the country unannounced. The natives do not know where they come from and do not know by what authority they are there. They do not know what the strangers want, and it is only natural that under such circumstances conflict should ensue.[64]

Of course, the above statement highlights the dichotomy between knowledge and ignorance created by Europeans, with their superior technology, in roaming the oceans and seas of the world

---
[63] British New Guinea, Report of 1886 by Special Commissioner, Queensland 1887, Appendix D.
[64] Brisbane Courier 6 August 1888 p 6.

looking for information, the unknown, land, trade goods, and trade itself. Europeans called this activity exploration and discovery. However, contact between unknown parties often led to conflict. Mercantile Europeans argued that the International Law of the Doctrine of Discovery gave them the right to occupy, settle, and erect colonies on any newfound land. Whereas, Exeter Hall followers frowned on these activities and sought to discourage interference with indigenous people. Modern schools of thought have arisen within colonised, metis communities who argue that the violent actions of their indigenous ancestors were not that of savages or barbarians against civilisation and advancement, but the exercise of lawful acts of military resistance to invasion.[65]

Table 1 below provides a list of marine incidents suffered by Europeans during the period of contact from 1859 up to the end of 1887 involving indigenous elements.[66] There were 48 incidents, 5 attacks on the Royal Navy, 8 attacks on missionaries, 22 attacks on fisheries, 7 attacks on traders and 6 attacks on explorers. Chart 1 represents the frequency of marine incidents for each group of foreigners as a percentage of the total number of marine incidents.

Chart 1

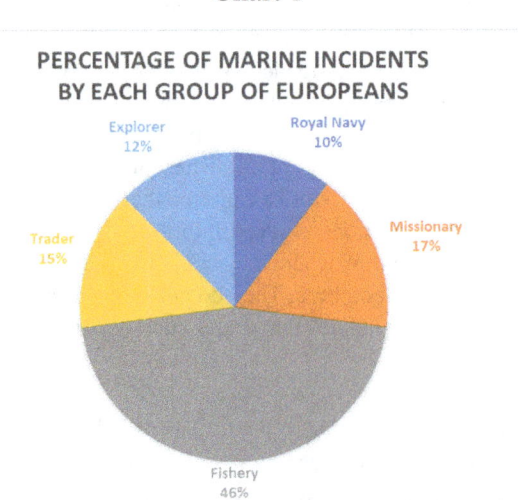

---

65 In Australia this school of thought is known as the Black Armband Brigade.
66 See pp 1414-116. The participants are identified as British subjects and Papuan natives, and the geographical location is broadly speaking the coastal zone of the south-east coast of New Guinea and adjacent islands.

ASSESSMENT

Arising out of the forty-eight marine incidents, one hundred and twenty-four deaths of non-Papuans occurred from physical violence by indigenous natives (Papuans), see Chart 2. These non-Papuan deaths were identified as follows:

Deaths per each European Group[67]

Royal Navy	Missionary	Fishery	Trader	Explorer
nil	6	91	20	7

Chart 2

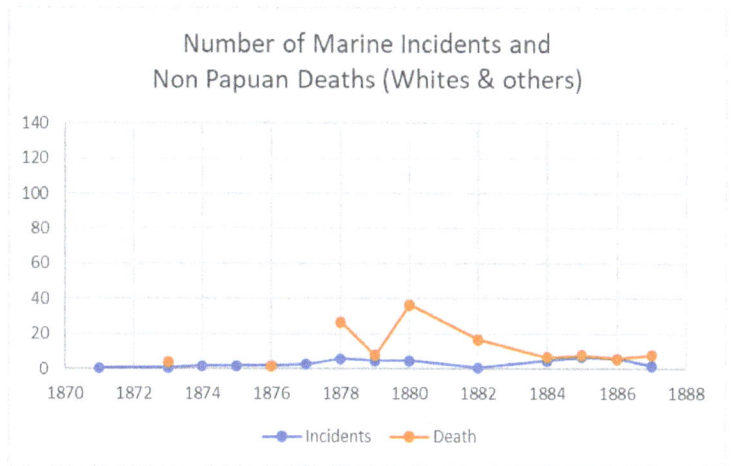

Chart 3

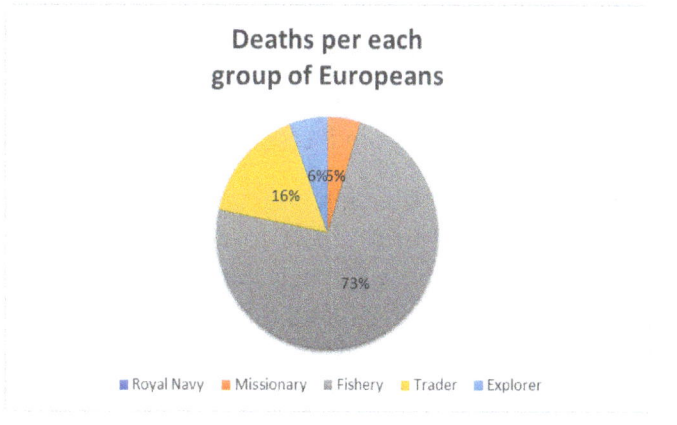

---

67 Note European in this context may include non-whites acting as servants or agents of whites.

The data in Table 1 might be better understood if the history of British New Guinea was viewed in the following manner:

1859 to 1877, terra incognito;

1878 to 1883, British supervision;

1884 to 1888, British protectorate;

1888 to Federation, British colony.

1859 to 1877 Terra Incognito.

In the southern coastal waters of New Guinea and adjacent islands, there was no recognised political system in control of the area; it was a lawless frontier. Therefore, foreigners and or indigenous natives were under no jurisdiction or control and thus, they were not accountable for the consequences of any outrage or offence they may have committed.

The data in Table 1 below indicate that in the decade commencing 1870, there were 10 incidents, 6 involving the LMS, 2 the Royal Navy, and 2 explorers. The data reflected the situation then existing on the ground. With the enactment of the Imperial Kidnapping Act of 1872, the Royal Navy began increased patrols in the South Sea Islands. Moreover, the LMS arrived in 1871 and were the only people actively operating and establishing bases in New Guinea. They owned and operated the vessel *Ellengowan,* which made frequent trips along the south coast of New Guinea, servicing and supplying existing mission stations as well as looking for future mission sites. This level of exposure to indigenous elements would increase the risk of attack from locals.

Captain J. Moresby, after his cruise in *Basilisk,* criticised the LMS. Moresby addressed a report to Mr. Murray, who was in charge of the LMS in New Guinea, on the state of the mission stations visited by *Basilisk*. He found that the Polynesian teachers placed on the Torres Strait Islands and New Guinea were left alone to fight a losing battle against famine, sickness, want of knowledge of the languages required, and the contempt and hostility of fierce

Papuan heathens. Moresby added that he had been glad to make himself useful in taking such supplies to them as Mr. Murray could provide. The circumstances of the teachers at Redscar, but for his visit and the abundant supplies he gave them, seemed that all would have perished. At Bampton Island, the two native teachers and their wives, who had been posted there some months previously, and had not been visited nor supplied, were murdered by the natives.[68]

Naturally, the LMS did not accept Moresby's criticism, and lengthy correspondence was conducted on the matter:

> With reference to Captain Moresby's reiterated charges, and strong statements relative to the teachers not being supplied, as he thinks they ought to be, with foreign food, perhaps it is hardly necessary that I should say more than I have said in my replies to his letters. He speaks from a very imperfect acquaintance with the circumstances. His opportunities for making personal observation were of course, very limited and some, at least of the sources from which he sought information, were of the most unsatisfactory character. In the course of the visitation which I have just completed, I have found nothing to bear out his strong statements, and from the teachers, I have had no complaints.[69]

The final incident involving the LMS was the attack on Captain Dudfield at South Cape on 28 December 1877. Mr. Goldie who came to the assistance of the gravely injured Dudfield, was greatly disturbed by the incident and in particular, Rev. J. Chalmers's apparent reckless disregard for his safety.[70] Goldie wrote:

> When I think on all the circumstances in connection with past and present arrangements of mission work down here, I feel indignant that a fraud of playing at mission work here should longer exist. I know for a fact that previous arrangements such as this had been made with the worthy missionary, the Rev. Mr. Lawes, and he can testify how little they have been attended to. I feel that I have a right to write on this matter, for I may be blamed for turning and leaving

---

68 Discoveries & Surveys, Moresby, 1876 p 166. Wagga Wagga Advertiser and Riverine Reporter 10 April 1872 p 3.
69 A.W. Murray, Cape York, March 11, 1873 https://nla.gov.au/nla.obj-2726815745/view
70 Rev. J. Chalmers was murder by natives in 1901 at Goaribari Island, Western District in circumstance of reckless disregard for own safety and that of others, see pp 105-110 below.

> Mr. Chalmers to his fate. When I would not have done so, even at the urgent entreaties of Captain Dudfield, though the explorer was certainly going to a deadly conflict if I had not thought that the mission steamer, which was at the time of our turning due at Port Moresby, would have been there. The *Mayri* was attacked on Saturday, 24 February 1877. We met her off Cape Rodney, on Tuesday, January 1, 1878, Andrew Goldie.[71]

J. P. Sunderland, Agent of the London Missionary Society, Sydney responded with a letter to the *Sydney Morning Herald*:

> He says, "When I think on all circumstances in connection with past and present arrangements of mission work done here, I feel indignant that a fraud of playing at mission work here should longer exist." This charge of fraud comes with ill-grace from one who has been kindly treated by the missionaries and native teachers belonging to the Missionary Society. Mr. Goldie knows that had it not been for the determination of Captain Turpie to remove Mr. Goldie from Port Moresby when he was very ill with fever, he would have died there. Is it a fraud that the London Missionary Society have established several stations in Torres Strait that the Rev. W. G. Lawes laboured at Port Moresby for upwards of two years, and, even according to Mr. Goldie, established a reputation far and wide as a good man? Is it a fraud that the Rev. J. Chalmers, an experienced missionary, has left his comfortable station in Rarotonga, and gone up to New Guinea to do what he can for the people of that great land? Is it a fraud that Mr Chalmers and his noble wife faced the excited tribes at South Cape, soothing their anger and removing their callousness, that they may ultimately make them understand their benevolent designs? Is it a fraud that men in obedience to what they consider to be the command of Christ, go to these places, face danger, endure hardships that they may be the means of elevating men in the scale of being? No, it is no fraud.[72]

For the sake of clarity in this study, I reiterate that this study relates to marine incidents. It may be of interest to the reader that Mr. A. Musgrave made a study of the mortality of Polynesian teachers employed by the LMS in New Guinea. Musgrave found that out of a total number of 187 Polynesians of both sexes, introduced from the Savage Islands, Loyalty Islands, &c., ninety succumbed to disease or the hostility of the natives. Of the latter, twelve were

---

71 Queanbeyan Age 9 March 1878 p 3.
72 Sydney Morning Herald 7 March 1878 p 5.

massacred.[73]

The next important group were the explorers and specimen collectors. By definition, these people were risk-takers, and it would be difficult to make judgments about collisions with indigenous elements because of the presumption of trespass by the explorer. However, indigenous elements were assumed to forego violence toward bona fide travellers and explorers. This brings me to the Royal Navy, where navigation, surveying and cartography were seen as part of the freedom of passage that all vessels have over the seas.

1878 to 1883 British Supervision.

The apparent random selection of 1878 as a start date for the next group of marine incidents was dictated by the commencement of the Western Pacific Order-in-Council of 1877. The Western Pacific Order-in-Council was of limited scope, only giving the High Commissioner jurisdiction over British subjects.[74] The Royal Navy was used as a de facto police force to keep the peace and good order. In practical terms of law enforcement, the High Commissioner had limited manpower and assets. In the matter of Captain Webb's alleged killing of a native boy, Sir G. W. Des Voeux, High Commissioner said, … "except through ships of war, I have no means of accomplishing an object of this kind, and I am compelled therefore either to apply to you for assistance or to leave its accomplishment unattempted".[75] From 1878 to 1883, there were 18 marine incidents. In 1878, 6 marine incidents resulted in 27 deaths, in 1879, 5 marine incidents with 8 deaths, and in 1880, 5 marine incidents with 37 deaths. In 1882, there was a marine incident in which a European killed a native and wounded another.

---

73 British New Guinea, Report for 1888, Queensland 1889, Appendix E, p 18. FIFE, WAYNE. "THE BAMPTON ISLAND MURDERS: EXPLORING THE HUMAN FACE OF COLONIALISM IN EARLY PAPUA." The Journal of the Polynesian Society, vol. 107, no. 3, 1998, pp. 263–86. JSTOR, http://www.jstor.org/stable/20706811. Accessed 14 Dec. 2022.
74 See sections 6 and 7 of the Pacific Islanders Protection Act 1875 (Imperial).
75 Records of Stations and Fleets/Series ADM 122/File 8. AJCP Reel No: 2704/New Guinea http://nla.gov.au/nla.obj-2007336172 images 216-218.

On 3 June 1878, J. Mullens, Foreign Secretary of the London Missionary Society, wrote to the Colonial Office as follows:

> 1. On various occasions the London Missionary Society have represented to Lord Carnarvon the perils to which the natives of New Guinea have recently been exposed by the schemes of adventurers, and they had the satisfaction of being assured by Lord Carnarvon that the Pacific Islanders Protection Act was for the protection of the natives from wrong.
>
> 3. The Directors, therefore, invite your kindest attention to the danger which has arisen; and they request that everything may be done both to secure protection to native rights and native life and help to our people in the sickness and privation to which they are exposing themselves.[76]

On 28 June 1878, the Colonial Office wrote to the Admiralty requesting the stationing of a man-of-war at Port Moresby to keep the peace of the gold rush and to determine whether the rush was sustainable.[77] The Admiralty replied on 5 July 1878 that *HMS Sappho* had been sent to New Guinea as requested, and Commander Digby was appointed a deputy commissioner at Port Moresby by Sir Arthur Gordon.[78]

HMS Sappho, during her patrol of the southern coastal waters of New Guinea from June to August 1878, investigated 3 marine incidents of 1878 and 1 marine incident from 1877. The 1877 incident involved the attack and serve wounding of Captain Dudfield of the *Mayri* at South Cape. Commander Digby found that peace had been restored and took no action against the natives other than to warn them of the consequences of killing white men.

HMS Sappho visited Brooker Island, the scene of the Redlich/McCort massacre, but did not land any officers or crew; nor take any steps to recover the property left there, believing that Captain Redlich's partner, McCort and his party, were the aggressors and that the natives had the best claim upon the plunder. The particulars of the visit of the *Sappho* were not made public, but great annoyance

---

76 C. 3617, p 29.
77 C. 3617 p 33.
78 C. 3617 pp 34 & 38.

was felt by Captain Redlich's friends that no effort was made to save the valuable lot of fish (bêche-de-mer) still on the island. Captain Redlich was at Port Moresby and did not see the Captain of the *Sappho*, but at Thursday Island, Mr. Goldie interviewed him on Captain Redlich's behalf; he declined, however, to take any further action.[79] Commander Digby of the *Sappho* drew the ire of the *Australian Town and Country Journal* of 25 January 1879:

> There ought to be no hesitation on the part of the naval authorities in promptly punishing these miserable wretches. Whatever may have been the initial cause of their hostility to the whites, the subjects of Her Majesty must be protected; and if repeated massacres are allowed to remain unpunished, even for a few months, no trader will be safe from the treachery of the more debased tribes. The whole of this melancholy story illustrates very strikingly the necessity, which we have often urged, of more effective representation of the Imperial Government among these islanders. The people of Northern Queensland, who admired Mr. Ingham for his courage and many good qualities, are now crying out for the *Spitfire*, an old pilot boat at Cooktown, to be equipped, and despatched to execute justice.[80]

The next incident that brought the presence of the Royal Navy was the massacre of the *Voura's* captain, W.B. Ingham and crew at Brooker Island. The visit of *HMS Cormorant* to Brooker Island was said to have been quite useless. The natives sent an insulting message to the captain through the interpreter threatening that they would kill every European who landed on the island. A few shells and rockets were fired, but no effort was made to land or to punish Mr. Ingham's murderers.[81]

The *Brisbane Courier* made the following comments in its editorial of 7 June 1879:

> The position and responsibilities of the commanders of HM's cruisers, commissioned to suppress irregularities or inflict punishment among the natives of these islands, has consequently been invested with peculiar difficulty. Urged on the one hand by excited cries for vengeance from relatives or survivors of

---

79 Morning Bulletin 18 Jul 1878 p 4.
80 Australian Town and Country Journal 25 January 1879 p 16.
81 Brisbane Courier 13 May 1879 p 2.

Europeans massacred by treachery, yet on the other, restrained by the knowledge that every instance of retributive justice will raise the shrieking exaggerations of Exeter Hall.[82] If Captain Blakesley's statement published by us yesterday, respecting the visit of *HMS Cormorant* to Brooker Island, is in accordance with facts, it is to be feared that Captain Bruce has very much erred on the side of leniency and has secured the contempt of the natives for our power to chastise their misdeeds. The representative of her Majesty's navy warned off the shore by four determined savages, armed with the rifles they had stolen, is a humiliating one, and the shelling of a few grass huts, called a village, by way of punishing a most treacherous massacre and asserting the might of Great Britain in these waters, from a safe distance, seems a pitiful exhibition of impotent anger well calculated to produce in the native mind precisely the results described by Captain Blakesley.[83]

The Chief Judicial Commissioner to the Western Pacific High Commission wrote as follows:

> In 1879, your Excellency may remember, we resolved to give these islanders a "severe lesson." They had killed Mr. Ingham and the crew of his small steamer; and, when the Commodore arrived here in your absence to consult upon Western Pacific matters, I cordially agreed with him that they should be punished. He went up in the *Wolverine*, surrounded the island by night with his boats in very rough weather, and did all that possibly could be done to ensure success. But one canoe only was taken, and two of the natives shot; the bulk of them escaped; and the houses and many cocoanut trees burned.[84]

The next outrage of significance was the murder of Irons and Willis, two white men who had ventured to New Guinea as cedar getters. These men were killed in circumstances of cold-blooded brutality. It was argued that they had ignored sound advice about the dangers of their enterprise but had nevertheless gone ahead with the foolhardy expedition. *HMS Beagle* was tasked with investigating the interference by natives with the LMS vessel *Ellengowan* at South Cape before proceeding to Cloudy Bay to investigate the murder of Irons and Willis. After that incident, the *Beagle* returned

---

82 The phrase "Exeter Hall" became a metonym for the abolitionist lobby, native sympathiser.
83 Brisbane Courier 7 June 1879 p 4, abridged.
84 PMB_1214-15, pdf.

to Cloudy Bay in November 1879 to investigate the attack on the schooner *Pride of the Logan* when 7 persons were killed.

In July 1880, seven Chinese crew of the junk *Sin O Ney* were murdered at Paramana Point. On 2 October, *HMS Conflict* visited New Guinea to investigate the capture of the Chinese junk and the murder of seven of the crew. It was reported that *Conflict* was forbidden to use force on the New Guinea natives who killed the crew of the Chinese junk; it was considered that they had provoked their fate by their conduct towards the natives.[85]

Following on from this incident, was the *Annie Brooks* which was attacked at Mewstone Island and her crew of seven Europeans and seven Chinese murdered. It was further learned that a group of French naturalists collecting in the vicinity of Moresby Island had also been massacred.

On 25 November 1880, at Cooktown, a public meeting was held to consider the news lately received from New Guinea concerning the murders perpetrated by the natives. The hall was draped in black, and there was a very large attendance, the mayor presiding. Resolutions were passed expressing indignation and horror at the recent atrocities in New Guinea, and urging the Government to take immediate steps to punish the murderers, and thus prevent future outrages; that it was necessary for the protection of life and property that a permanent naval force should be stationed on the coast of New Guinea with more discretionary power vested in naval commanders. It was emphasised that thirty Europeans, besides Chinese and Kanakas, had been murdered during the last three years from Cooktown alone, and that property to the value of about £12,000 had been destroyed by the Papuans during the same period. A resolution was also passed to the effect that the French Consul at Sydney be informed of the murder of M. Naudan and his party, all of whom were residents of Cooktown. The inaction of the British war schooner was strongly condemned, though this was attributed to outside influences.[86]

---

85 Queenslander 13 November 1880 p 613.
86 Maryborough Chronicle, Wide Bay and Burnett Advertiser 27 November 1880 p 2.

The French, in response to the murder of Naudan and his colleagues, sent the *Croiseur d'Estree* to New Guinea, which landed an armed contingent, and destroyed 118 houses and all the plantations they could find, as well as shooting several natives.

The straw that broke the camel's back came in October 1880, when the schooner *Prosperity* returning from five months fishing, with a large cargo of bêche-de-mer, was plundered and afterwards burnt. Sir Arthur Kennedy, Governor of Queensland, wrote to the Commodore of the Australian station, respecting the reported massacres at New Guinea, only to receive from Commodore J. C. Wilson in late January 1881, the following:

> I have to inform your Excellency that it is impossible to detail a ship at this time specially for this case. The *Emerald*, however, which is at present engaged in the islands, is under orders to inquire into, and deal with, any cases that may come under her notice.[87]

In fact, in December 1880, Commodore J. C. Wilson had already issued sailing orders to Captain W. H. Maxwell of the *Emerald* to proceed to the scene of the murder of Lt. Bower and five crew of *Sandfly* and inflict serve punishment on the murderers and then to inquire into the *Ripple, Esperanza* and *Borealis* and severely punish the offenders. Maxwell was also directed to investigate the *Annie Brooks* matter and any cases he should hear of and deal with them as "you think fit and just."[88]

On 31 January 1881, Captain Maxwell of *HMS Emerald* at Sydney reported to Commodore Wilson regarding his cruise to investigate and punish the various outrages he had been tasked to take action against. Maxwell followed up on the *Annie Brooks* incident by speaking with relevant witnesses to the incident. He visited Brooker Island, Mewstone Island and the surrounding area and carried out a systematic scorched earth policy of burning villages, destroying canoes and cutting downs fruit trees. However, he was unable to catch and punish any natives. Maxwell appeared

---

Sydney Mail and New South Wales Advertiser 11 December 1880 p 1120. Brisbane Courier 25 November 1880 p 3.
87 Albury Banner and Wodonga Express 25 February 1881 p 15.
88 PMB 1214 Vol 17 p 1.

to have received news of the *Prosperity* incident but did not act on it.

The *Brisbane Courier* published a lengthy report on the cruise of *HMS Emerald* to the Solomon Islands to investigate the attacks on *HMS Sandfly, Ripple, Esperanza and Borealis*. In the same edition of the paper, a rather scathing editorial was also published denouncing the lack of action by the Australian station in suppressing massacres in the South Seas:

> In reply to a letter from his Excellency Sir Arthur Kennedy, calling attention to the massacre of the crew of the schooner *Prosperity*, Commodore Wilson regrets that he cannot detail a ship specially for this case, but anticipates that the *Emerald* will do all that is necessary. It looks as though the Commodore thought that the cruise of one of Her Majesty's ships among the islands would entirely satisfy everybody.
>
> The proceedings of *HMS Emerald* read almost like a clever satire on the method of inflicting official vengeance. If the author of *Pinafore* could only get hold of the details of this cruise, he might, by putting Sir Joseph Porter in command of the *Emerald*, make another hit as happy as his former naval romance. The *Emerald* appears to have passed from group to group impotently demonstrating, doing a little shell practice occasionally at distant villages, sometimes, as is proudly chronicled in the log, making an excellent shot, the shell bursting in an empty village. The bluejackets constantly land, and when they can get anyone to show them through the bush, make their way to some inland village and burn the grass gunyahs. When they are unable to get a pathfinder, they cut down a few cocoanut trees, burn any canoes that may be lying about and pass on to the scene of some other bygone massacre to repeat these tactics. The natives, who have been watching the whole thing securely from their scrub refuge, then probably emerge from their hiding places and celebrate the termination of the excitement with a war dance, and the next day's labour suffices to repair the damage done by the terrible visitor.
>
> The proceedings of the *Emerald* have been published opportunely, inasmuch as they strongly confirm what has been stated by the inter-colonial delegates in their memorial. Perhaps, therefore, although barren of present tangible results, the cruise will lead to reforms in Pacific administration which will render the property and lives of

British subjects in the South Seas more secure.[89]

The Inter-colonial Conference of 1881 commenced on 13 January. On 19 January, Mr. A. Palmer, of Queensland, moved, "That in the opinion of this Conference, it is desirable that a representation be made to Her Majesty the Queen, calling her attention to the lamentable state of affairs existing between the natives of many of the islands in the Pacific and the subjects of Her Majesty trading in those seas, more particularly since the appointment of a High Commissioner for the Pacific, and praying that Her Majesty will cause such action to be taken as will prevent the recurrence of such outrages against life and property as have lately prevailed."[90]

The Inter-colonial Conference agreed to the following resolutions, among others:

> 2. That more effectual means should be devised for the punishment of natives of the said islands for any crimes or offences committed by them against British subjects.
>
> 4. That the more frequent visits of her Majesty's ships among the islands should tend to lessen in a great degree the crimes now so prevalent.

It is worth noting that the Hon. A. Palmer, Premier of Queensland, received the following telegram while attending the Inter-colonial Conference in Sydney.

> Crew of schooner *Prosperity*, owned by myself, murdered and vessel and cargo burnt at Leocadie Island near South Cape, New Guinea, October or November last; Captain alone supposed has escaped; value property destroyed, thirteen hundred; eight men murdered, making during last six months thirty-one men murdered from Cooktown alone, and five thousand property destroyed; no action appears contemplated by Imperial Government, protect the trade; our men dare not effect reprisals or attack beforehand which is often the only way of preventing massacres. What can be done? As Mr. Palmer is in Sydney, please get him use influence to have murderers of *Annie Brooks* and *Prosperity's* crew properly punished; no provocation this time alleged for either massacre.

---

89   Brisbane Courier 15 February 1881 p 2.
90   Argus 29 January 1881 p 9, abridged.

William J. Hartley.[91]

Sir A. Gordon, High Commissioner for the Western Pacific, rejected these aspersions against the Western Pacific administration and launched into a lengthy defence of his administration as follows:

> The charge preferred against the High Commissioner is twofold. It is alleged that he has, on the one hand, shown undue leniency towards the misdeeds of natives, and, on the other, has shown equally undue harshness in the punishment of British subjects when charged before him with offences against natives. The jurisdiction of the High Commissioner extends over all British subjects in the Western Pacific but over British subjects exclusively. He has no authority whatever to deal, whether judicially or in his executive capacity, with the offences of natives of islands not under the dominion of the Crown. The High Commissioner has on more than one occasion pointed out to the Imperial Government that, unless a jurisdiction were created competent to take cognisance of offences committed against British subjects in the Pacific beyond Her Majesty's possessions, the infliction of punishment on British subjects for outrages against natives was sure to excite on their part a sense of being treated with injustice. The reply returned to such representations has invariably been that in the opinion of the Law Officers of the Crown insuperable obstacles exist to any assumption of jurisdiction by Her Majesty, over others than British subjects, beyond the limits of Her Majesty's dominions. Therefore, the High Commissioner is absolutely powerless to take judicial cognisance of any offence committed by a Polynesian native not also a subject of Her Majesty.
>
> Conference should not have allowed itself to be made a medium for the dissemination of slanders on men holding high and responsible situations, who had received no intimation of the intentions of the Conference to investigate the nature of the functions committed to them by the Crown.[92]

In the matter of Capt. Webb of the *Pride of the Logan* on 24 July 1882, at Bootless Inlet, New Guinea killing one native and wounding another, it was taken up by Commodore J. E. Erskine of

---

91 Minutes of proceedings of the Intercolonial Conference held at Sydney, January, 1881.
92 PMB 1214 Vol 9 p 36, abridged.

the Australian station with much vigour.

Cooktown, 24 August 1882, Messrs. J. Chalmers & W. Lawes wrote to Commodore Erskine making a complainant against Capt. Webb, *Pride of the Logan* that at Bootless Inlet, on 24 July 1882, he fired on the natives and killed one and wounded another.

Nelson at Sydney, 29 September 1882, Erskine wrote to Governor A. E. Kennedy advising Messrs. Lawes & Chalmers had made a complaint against Capt. Webb, *Pride of the Logan* for an outrage against natives of Bootless Inlet.

Fiji, 13 October 1882, Governor G. W. Des Voeux wrote to Erskine Re Capt. Webb, for the assistance of the Royal Navy to bring Webb to justice before the Judicial Commissioner of the Western Pacific.

Nelson at Sydney, 14 April 1883, Erskine wrote to Governor A. E. Kennedy Re Capt. Webb. Now that Webb had returned to Cooktown, the allegations against Webb should be investigated by Queensland authorities.

Brisbane, 21 May 1883, A. H. Palmer Administrator wrote to Erskine Re Capt. Webb. Qld Attorney-General advised insurmountable difficulties in obtaining a conviction against Webb. The matter better handled by the High Commissioner for the Western Pacific.

Fiji, 29 June 1883, Governor Des Voeux wrote to Erskine Re Webb. As High Commissioner for the Western Pacific, Des Voeux advised Erskine he wished to proceed against Webb and asked Erskine to make a ship available to apprehend Webb.

Nelson at Fiji, 7 July 1883, Erskine wrote to Governor Des Voeux Re Capt. Webb. Erskine advised Des Voeux he had no ships available, but he would do all he could to bring the offender to justice.

Capt. Webb was never apprehended by the Royal Navy but on or about July or August 1884, Capt. Webb and his wife were murdered by the blacks at Millport Bay, New Guinea.[93]

In 1882, a wreck, possibly the *Tavioni*, was found at the mouth of the Fly. There were no survivors, and inquiries with the local natives revealed that the crew had been killed and their heads taken.

1884 to 1888 — British Protectorate

The next event of significance in the advancement of New Guinea was the establishment of the British Protectorate. When the Protectorate was established in 1884, the proclamation read:

> Whereas it has become essential, for the protection of the lives and properties of the native inhabitants of New Guinea, and for the purpose of preventing the occupation of portions of that country by persons whose proceedings, unsanctioned by any lawful authority, might tend to injustice, strife, and bloodshed, and who, under the pretence of legitimate trade and intercourse, might endanger the liberties and possess themselves of the lands of such native inhabitants, that a British Protectorate should be established.[94]

The Protectorate merely defined the jurisdiction of British influence, and provided for the establishment of an administration, a commissioner and staff, for the control and regulation of British subjects within the jurisdiction. Foreign nationals and indigenous natives were outside the jurisdiction. However, the Royal Navy continued to be employed as a de facto law enforcement agency. The Protectorate was declared on 6 November 1884 together with the appointment of a special commissioner for the Protectorate, Major General P. H. Scratchley, who served from 22 November 1884 to 2 December 1885, dying in office.

During Scratchley's tenure, the following cases were investigated:

> The charge of robbery with violence upon Dan Rowan, committed by the natives at Aroma. The killing of Captain Miller, at Normanby

---

93 Records of Stations and Fleets/Series ADM 122/File 8. AJCP Reel No: 2704/New Guinea http://nla.gov.au/nla.obj-2007340761 images 200-217.
94 GG VOL. XXXV.] 23 December 1884. [No. 113, p 2037.

Island; the killing of Reid, at Slade Island; the killing of Captain Frier, at Moresby Island; the killing of Bob Lumse at Hayter Island; the killing of Captain Webb at Millport Bay in 1884; the attack on the schooner Wild Duck, in Cloudy Bay, in June 1884.[95]

On 2 October 1885, P. H. Scratchley, Special Commissioner for the protected territory of New Guinea published the following notice in the Queensland government gazette:

> Portions of coast unsafe to Traders and others.
>
> Traders and others are cautioned against visiting the following portions of the coast and islands in the Protectorate: From Kerepunu to South Cape (including Moresby Island), D'Entrecasteaux Group, Engineer Group, Woodlark Group, Jurien and Jouvency islands; also, from East Cape to the German boundary on the northeast coast.[96]

In the period 1886 to 1887, during the tenure of John Douglas, 8 marine incidents occurred with 14 deaths as follows. In 1886, 3 whites and 5 Malays were killed at Joannet Island by local natives. In 1886, 6 Chinese crew were killed at Moresby Island, and 2 whites were killed at Orangerie Bay.

During the period of the British Protectorate, the Royal Navy became very active in enforcing Pax Britannica. On 2 April 1886, Rear Admiral Tryon wrote to the Admiralty, regarding cases in the islands of Western Pacific, dealt with by Her Majesty's Ships in 1885. He said Sir Peter Scratchley wrote to him to say how indebted he felt for the assistance rendered him by Captain Clayton, (*HMS Diamond*) and expressed his high opinion of Clayton's judgment. Scratchley also wrote, under date 13 November 1885, on the subject of those who were sent "to collect bêche-de-mer, &c., in vessel unsuitable for the work, insufficiently manned, and worked in a manner that could end in only one way, i.e., the killing, sooner or later, of the wretched masters and crews." He considered that "licenses for such trade should only be given to properly manned

---
95 Fort, G. Seymour & Scratchley, Peter. (1886). British New Guinea: report on British New Guinea, from data and notes by the late Sir Peter Scratchley, Her Majesty's Special Commissioner, Melbourne p 6 & 12.
96 GG VOL. XXXVII.] 2 October 1885. [No. 59 p 1163.

and found vessels." Tryon went on to say, the difficulty in dealing with outrage cases was the fact that the tribes were very numerous in the islands, and by the absence of recognised chiefs. It was in the tribal or family capacity that action was taken by them, and it was this that made it difficult to apply a modern system of civilisation and law. To have the same deterrent effect on Papuan races as it had on those who belong to civilised nations, a few years of patience and firmness, with moderation, would doubtless do much, and would soon stop the action of these savage races whose customs and traditions embrace the killing of a man for the sake of his head, or for other wanton reasons.

Set out below are the cases dealt with by the Royal Navy:

> Murder of Captain Webb, his wife, one Malay, and two Australians (Natives), and the destruction of cutter *Marion*, by natives, at Millport Harbour, New Guinea, in January 1885. *HMS Diamond*, at Port Moresby, 1 November 1885. In continuation of my report of 25 October, every effort was made to communicate with the natives, but without effect. I, therefore, threw a few shells into the villages on the hill and destroyed five canoes and some nets.
>
> Death at the hands of natives of William Reed, at Tupi Tupi or Slade Island, one of the Engineer Group, in January 1885. It would seem that the unfortunate man was very much to blame. I propose, if possible, visiting the island again, when I may be able to see the chief, also Alloopatoo and Makisoka; but it does not appear to me to be a case for severe punishment.
>
> Death at the hands of natives of Frank Gerret, a Trader, and master of the ketch *P.T.M.* at Deboyne Island, Louisiade Archipelago, New Guinea, on 31 January 1885. I therefore did not punish anyone and beg to refer the case for your consideration. I recovered the skull of the deceased man, which will be buried at sea.
>
> Death at the hand of natives of Bob Lumse, a Malay, a Trader at Magaikarona, Hayter Island, China Straits, New Guinea, in February 1885. On his return, his Excellency (Scratchley) informed me that the murder has doubtless been committed and that trade disputes had caused it; but he did not see how any further steps could be taken, the murderers being absent, and the chief and other villagers having had nothing to do with the matter.

Murder of Captain Fryer, Master and Owner, John Watkins, Carpenter, and two natives (one South Sea Islander, and one Queensland boy), belonging to the schooner *Lalla Rookh*, by natives at Hoop Iron Bay, Moresby Island, New Guinea, about 25-29 July 1885. *Diamond*, at sea, 16 December 1885. I destroyed the village, which contained some of the best houses I have seen in New Guinea. Doubtless, this destruction will be a severe punishment, but not too severe for the treacherous and unprovoked murder of the master and carpenter of the *Lalla Rookh*.

Murder of Captain Miller, a Trader, of the cutter *Daisy* on 3 October 1885, on Ventenat Island, off S.E. Point of Normanby Island, D'Entrecasteaux Group, New Guinea. After firing three shells to clear the bush, I landed four boats' crews from *Diamond*, two from *Raven*, and destroyed three villages, bringing off three canoes and several fishing nets which were too wet to burn. No trees or growing crops were injured.[97]

As to the Craig case, Joannet Island, John Douglas reported the matter to Admiral Tryon. Mr. Forbes, the Resident Officer, Samarai, reported to Captain Clayton, of *HMS Diamond*. On 20 November, Captain Clayton, in the *Diamond*, visited the scene of the massacre but could do nothing, for the offending natives had taken to the impenetrable bush.

After consultation by John Douglas with Captain Clayton, and with his approval, Douglas arranged for Forbes to re-visit Jonnnet to recover the arms and ammunition taken from the *Emily*. Forbes was, on the whole, successful in recovering some of the firearms and ammunition. However, press reports suggested that Nicholas Minister employed by Douglas to assist Forbes on his return visit had shot several natives and cut off their heads, which were displayed as trophies. The matter became the subject of a question in the Victorian Legislative Assembly on 20 July 1887.[98]

---

[97] Papers relative to Armed Reprisals inflicted upon Natives of various Islands in the Western Pacific by *HMS Diamond*, GB PP, 1886, 51-Sess. 2.
[98] British New Guinea: report for the year 1887, Victoria, 1888 Appendix J p 41. Griffith, Samuel & Forbes, Henry O & Douglas, John & Gillies, Duncan. (1887). Massacres in British New Guinea: http://nla.gov.au/nla.obj-3105134958 HC Command Papers C. 5883 p 128.

In the case of the Chinese crew at Moresby Island, John Douglas reported on 31 December 1887 as follows:

> Early in the year, the *Pride of the Logan* schooner from Cooktown got on shore in Mudge Bay on Moresby Island, not far from Samarai. Her crew, consisting of six Chinamen, were killed by the natives, and the vessel was cut to pieces. This caused very strained relations with the inhabitants of Moresby Island and led to some reprisals being made by Captain Musgrave in *HMS Rapid*. He visited them more than once. They admitted their fault, sued for peace, and they have lately been on friendly terms with us, occasionally visiting Samarai.[99]

1888 to Federation, British Colony.

The final period in the study is from 4 September 1888 to Federation when the Crown colony of British New Guinea was erected. The colony and everything in it, including the indigenous population, became subjects of the Queen. The Queen appointed an Administrator to govern the colony with full executive and legislative powers, subject to Her disallowance. The natives became British subjects and were therefore subject to the control and regulation of the Administrator.

Turning now to marine incidents that occurred within the jurisdiction of the colony of British New Guinea, the first relevant marine incident occurred in October 1888 when the *Star of Peace* was attacked by natives at Chads Bay. Captain Edward Ansell was killed by the natives and his vessel ransacked of its goods and trade and then burnt.

Pursuant to the laws of British New Guinea, on 18 January 1889, eleven persons were put on trial at the Central Court sittings at Samarai, for the murder of Ansell and stealing in a ship. Of these, four were convicted of the murder of Ansell and sentenced to capital punishment, five were convicted of stealing and sentenced to imprisonment for twelve months, likewise, one to imprisonment

---

[99] British New Guinea: report for the year 1887, Victoria, 1888 p 9.

for eighteen months, and one was acquitted. The four natives sentenced to death were executed by hanging. One prisoner (Wobba-wobbina) was executed at Samurai, on 28 January 1889; one (Hannu-wannu) at Abioma, in Milne Bay, on 29 January 1889; and two (Igwarri-gohoi, Tutina-wai) at Chads Bay on 30 January 1889.

In 1898, the chief judicial officer of British New Guinea published a report showing for the last ten years, that 128 natives had been convicted of murder by the Central Court, but only eleven had been executed. Of these, nine were convicted of murdering Europeans, one of murdering a Chinese, and one of murdering a native constable.[100]

The sentence imposed on the native convicted at Dobu, on 23 December 1891, was for the murder of an honest, industrious, inoffensive Chinese settler, who had been resident in the country for many years. He lived like a European and was regarded by the natives as being a white man. As nothing could be found to mitigate the gravity of the offence, the sentence was carried into effect in the district of the prisoner, where the murder was committed.[101]

The reason why so few natives were executed was that the motive for the killing justified the murder from a native point of view. The Administration acknowledged this dimension of the crime and, therefore, considered it perfectly equitable to regard it as a sufficient palliation to warrant a commutation of the sentence.

The following conclusions might be drawn from the above policy. In cases of black-on-black violence, where the black offender was convicted of murder and sentenced to death, his sentence was commuted to penal servitude. When a black offender was convicted of the murder of a European and sentenced to death, he was executed as a deterrent to killing white men.[102]

---

100 British New Guinea, Report for 1 July 1897 to 30 June 1898, Queensland 1898, Appendix J p 70.
101 British New Guinea, Report for 1 July 1891 to 30 June 1892, Queensland 1893, p XIV.
102 Papua: or, British New Guinea by Murray, John Hubert Plunkett, T. Fisher Unwin, London 1912 p 212, 234.

Chart 4[103]

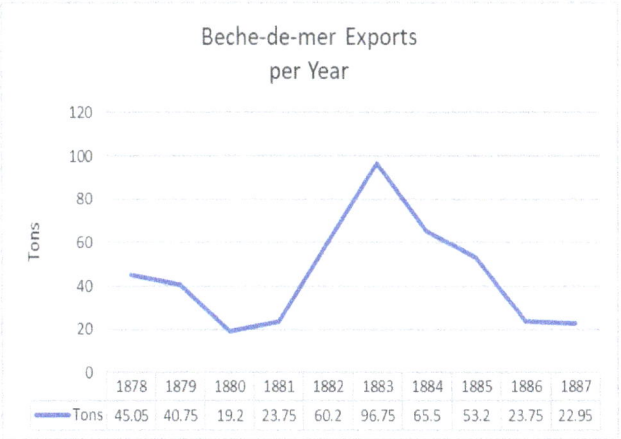

Table 1 reveals that the group with the highest number of marine incidents, as well as the highest fatalities while operating in and around New Guinea coastal waters and adjacent islands, was the Fishery group or bêche-de-mer fishers.

Chart 5

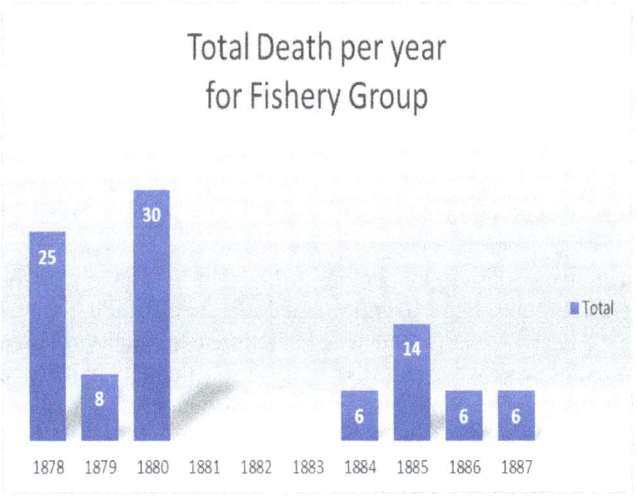

Of course, the substantive task is to determine whether any qualitative conclusions can be drawn from the data. One has only the white man's side of the story, and when each case was examined, it was found that, on occasion, the natives were

---

103 British New Guinea, Report for 1888, Queensland 1889, Appendix F p 33.

provoked. Sometimes a life was taken to pay for the life of a native who had died on the Queensland plantations or elsewhere; but at other times, no reason could be discovered, beyond a bloodlust or a desire for plunder. There is of course, the study made by the Hon. A. Musgrave, then Assistant Deputy Commissioner, *Return of Outrages and Massacres* and published in the Annual Report of 1886.[104] I quote Musgrave as follows:

> Our aborigines are savages in the first stages of barbarism, swayed by intense and degrading superstitions which involve them in ceaseless inter-tribal feuds and bloodshed, and the first protection that the natives require in British New Guinea is from each other. From one end of our territory to the other a chronic state of inter-tribal hostility prevails, and I much doubt if a day passes in the year without a murder or massacre (often of women and children) taking place in some district. No real tribal discipline or organisation exists, and to "govern by the natives" is a sheer impossibility.[105]

Commodore Wilson, writing to the secretary of the Admiralty on 5 July 1879, observed:

> Unprejudiced people cannot but have much sympathy for these tough hardy men, the true pioneers of trade and civilisation. No one admits that these lives as a rule are particularly moral or free from blame, but they are by no means more criminal or vicious than the average Englishmen. They are generally most liberal in their trading transactions, for self-interest makes them just in their treatment of the natives. Opinions at home touching traders are largely from missionary reports. Of course, the missionary and the traders are antagonistic, not but that amongst the better-informed churchmen, there are to be found liberal-minded men who would endorse my views, but as it stands, they can have little community of interests. He trades with what the missionary justly thinks is pernicious to the native, such as muskets, powder, and liquor, but the trader has no fine feeling on the subject; he wants certain articles and is ready to give what is asked for in exchange. Thus, the missionary is too ready to paint the trader as he appears to himself, forgetting that, in the eyes of the world, he would really, if fairly judged, be no worse, and probably considerably better than others of his own class and calling in civilised life.[106]

---

104 British New Guinea, Annual Report 1886, Queensland 1887, Appendix D p 17.
105 Ibid., p 25.
106 Item 04-Islands of the Western Pacific. Commodore Wilson to Secretary of

The following is taken from a report by the Rev. W. Lawes to Special Commissioner Scratchley on the natives of New Guinea:

> and as ready to resent interference with their women as civilised men. Remembering all this, I know of no case in which it can be said with certainty that the natives were the first aggressors. Instead of being described "savage," "hostile," and "treacherous," they should, in justice, be spoken of as kindly disposed and friendly on their first intercourse with white men, but generally suspicious and watchful. If we are to believe the boasts of men from New Guinea over their cups in Cooktown and Thursday Island, then there was nothing exceptional in the voyage of the *Hopeful* and its atrocities. The cupidity of the people has sometimes been excited by the quantity of goods possessed by the white man, but here their own customs must be remembered. No man can accumulate much more than his fellows, and they must give when asked.[107]

Musgrave documented eighty collisions between indigenous natives and Europeans, from 11 May 1845 to 30 June 1886. For the period 1859 to 1887, he identified 67 collisions. Of those incidents, Musgrave considered 6 to have been provoked by non-Papuans. All the remaining incidents were the result of unprovoked violence and murder on the part of indigenous Papuans.[108] Furthermore, I give great weight to Musgrave's study and conclusions not only because it was compiled on-the-spot by a creditable official with sufficient authority to access relevant documents and records, but Musgrave had the document vetted by Andrew Goldie, an equally creditable figure because of his longstanding association with British New Guinea. The 6 incidents or collisions alleged to have involved provocation by outsiders or Europeans were: Item 44, July 1878, *Annie* and *Pride of the Logan* at Keppel Point; item 45, 1878, McCourt at Brooker Island; item 55, 1880, murder of Chinese at Aroma; item 56, 1880, Mulholland at Cloudy Bay; item 65, 22 December 1884, Reed at Slade Island; and item 71, 29 July 1889, Frier at Moresby Island.

All the victims in the above six incidents were bêche-de-mer fishers. In Chart 5, the first returns for fish caught commenced

---
Admiralty, PMB_1214-04, pdf.
107 Ibid., p 25.
108 British New Guinea, Annual Report 1886, Queensland 1887, Appendix D p 17.

in 1878. On 21 January 1879, the Rev. W. Lawes wrote to Sir A. Gordon, High Commissioner for the Western Pacific as follows:

> The discovery of quantities of bêche-de-mer along the coast has already led to several vessels going from Australian ports. The men on board these vessels are of the worst character, and as they have their vessels to escape in there is but little self-interest to induce them to respect native rights. It is from these vessels that difficulties have already arisen with the natives, as reported in the colonial papers. I was resident for three years at Port Moresby and found the natives friendly and amenable to kindly treatment. I visited a great many villages, in most of which no white man had been before. I went along the coast as far as China Straits in our little mission steamer, calling at many places en route. In none of these journeys or voyages, was I molested.[109]

Sir Peter Scratchley, Special Commissioner for the protectorate of British New Guinea, noted in his diary as follows:

> Wednesday, October 7, 1885. I am satisfied that these traders are often reckless, unscrupulous, brutal, and piratical. They cheat the natives and are apt to appeal to their revolvers. I cannot feel any sympathy for such men. They go where they have no business to. They are a thorn in my side, and I do not think the life of any white man should be risked in avenging their deaths.[110]

The Rev. W. Lawes, Port Moresby, on 17 September 1885 wrote to the *Sydney Morning Herald* as follows:

> Papers just to hand bring us news of the killing of Captain Frier, at Hoop Iron Bay, Moresby Island. The press as a whole seems to take it for granted that the natives are entirely in the wrong and that righteousness and justice are entirely on our side, "Murder," "Massacres," and "Outrages," are the chosen headings for calling public attention to events into which no inquiry has been made, and no opportunity for explanation given.
>
> There are some states of society in which lynch law is justifiable. The same plea holds good for club law. There is no other known among the natives of New Guinea. White men who come to New Guinea must be prepared to run some risk in pursuit of the object they have in view. The climate of New Guinea is unhealthy, its

---

109 A & P C. 3617, Enclosure in No. 32, p 100.
110 Australian Defences and New Guinea compiled from papers of Peter Scratchley, by Kinloch-Cooke, Clement, London, Macmillan, 1887 p 337.

people barbarous, and its government club law.

I don't think there is one case which may not be attributed either to reckless disregard of warning or violation of native rights. Captains Webb and Frier, I know personally. The whole course of their lives and treatment of the natives was such that I am not the least surprised at the ending.

I could mention other cases where the intruder had caused things with a high hand until his career has been suddenly stopped. The public is horrified by another massacre but knows nothing of the line of conduct which has led up to it, and to which violent death is the natural sequel. The man Read, who was killed at Slade Island, is said to have provoked and irritated the natives by persistently following the women, &c. The ostensible reason for his death was his ill-treatment of the boy who ran away and hid himself in the bush and was believed by his friends to be dead.

I see there have been indignation meetings and a great cry for punishment. By all means; but let it fall upon the guilty men those who for love of greed violated the first principles of civilisation and inhumanity.[111]

The Rev. Lawes was answered by the well-known New Guinea explorer and writer T. F. Bevan[112] by a letter to the editor which appeared in the *Brisbane Courier* as follows:

Rev. W. Lawes, of Port Moresby, apologises on behalf of the native murderers of William Reid, Captain Webb, wife and party, Bob Lumse, Frank Gerret, Captain Frier, and Watkins, and of Captain Fred Miller.

Now audi alteram partem—from one of yourselves. The abovementioned massacres have all taken place, as Mr. Lawes well knows, not within "recent years," but within this "present" year; not before but all the time after the Mission were entrusted with interpreting and expounding to the natives of New Guinea that "club law" was once and forever superseded by "British law;" not when the country was destitute of war vessels, but while ships of war were passing near the very spots, and while those who have since been murdered were not—a plague on such insinuations—interfering

---
111 Sydney Morning Herald 6 October 1885 p 4, abridged.
112 H. J. Gibbney, 'Bevan, Theodore Francis (1860–1907)', Australian Dictionary of Biography, National Centre of Biography, Australian National University, https://adb.anu.edu.au/biography/bevan-theodore-francis-2991/text4371, published first in hardcopy 1969, accessed online 21 November 2022.

with native women or violating native rights, but were trembling in their shoes, having heard their own death knell. What time the unnoticed murder of William Reid took place at the Engineer Group in December last—say a month after the protectorate ceremony—and Mr. Chalmers, in *HMS Raven*, passed by near at hand a few days thereafter, and heard of, but heeded not, the first murder of the new series, and under the British protectorate, namely, murders for plunder, which the natives concluded could be enjoyed with impunity!

So much for Mr. Chalmers as an interpreter, and hater of white settlers! "Disregard of warning" and "violation of native rights" forsooth, and justification of "club law" on the extraordinary grounds that "there is no other law;" extraordinary because his Excellency is now holding his court in New Guinea.

But assuming that Mr. Lawes is correct, and that "club law" is "lord paramount," what, I would ask, would be done to the white man that exercised it, even in self-defence? Who made Messrs. Lawes and Chalmers judges over those murdered men? When do they reside in or what do they know of the east end of New Guinea, with their snug quarters, solely in Port Moresby, save what they are told by men of colour, who say what they are wanted to say?

And—mark the amazing anomaly—nothing has angered the Mission more than because some have said that the natives have never been made to understand the true character of the protectorate, and nevertheless, a year nearly after the mission were entrusted with interpreting the proclamation of "British law," Mr. Lawes, writing in the *Sydney Morning Herald*, says, on 6 October last in effect of New Guinea: "Its Government is "club law," and it has no other law." If such a statement does not involve gross disrespect to our indefatigable and popular, but sadly hampered Governor, his Excellency Sir Peter H. Scratchley, and disloyalty to Queen and country, I am at a loss to know what would! At all events, its tone will give some idea to the British public generally with what deep felt detestation the Mission is regarded by settlers in New Guinea.[113]

Chart 5 indicates that in the period 1885-1886, twenty deaths of bêche-de-mer fishers were recorded at the hands of Papuans. These fatalities generated a good deal of notoriety and criticism of the protectorate's failure to protect white men and their crews fishing and trading along the south coast of New Guinea. J. Douglas,

---

113 Brisbane Courier 19 January 1886 p 6, abridged.

Special Commissioner for New Guinea, reported that the valuable pearlshell and bêche-de-mer fisheries were now abandoned on account of the numerous murders of those engaged in them, and it was no longer safe for a white man to show his face on the coast.[114]

The qualitative analysis suggests that the LMS and Scratchley believed the cause of the collisions between Europeans and Papuans was a result of the Europeans and their non-white servants provoking the Papuans by breaching their customs, manners and etiquette. The major breaches appeared to be sexual abuse of Papuan women, deceptive trade practices,[115] and disrespect for cultural sensitivities.

DISRESPECT FOR CULTURAL SENSITIVITIES.

Chart 6 sets out the locations where Europeans were killed by Papuans. The geographical area having the largest number of fatalities was the southeast of British New Guinea. During 1884, Queensland labour vessels recruited labourers from this area, especially from Mewstone Island and Moresby Island. A Royal Commission found that the natives taken from this area had been duped and had never consented to be employed on the cane fields of Queensland as labourers. The Queensland government returned them to their home islands. It seems that through bureaucratic bungling, not all labourers were returned, and in the case of deceased labourers, not all family members were compensated with blood money (wergild). These families and their relatives went unrecompensed and naturally bore a grudge against the white man.

In the native mind, all white men belonged to one tribe and, therefore, were jointly and severally liable for the actions of other white men. However, white men did not need to offer a head as compensation but could pay a fine instead of the wergild (a head).

---

114 British New Guinea, Report for 1886, Special Commissioner, Queensland 1887 p 8.
115 Under paying, not paying, over charging, failing to keep a bargain made, defective goods, etc.

Mr. Romilly, Deputy Commissioner, put it this way:

> it becomes a matter between natives and white men; it is not held to be absolutely necessary that a white man's head must be procured before the unquiet spirit can be laid. Heavy payment in trade goods will answer the same purpose. During the last two years, two of the murders committed in the south-east, were probably by this omission. As there was no prospect of obtaining compensation, the natives had to take the first white heads they could procure.[116]

The catch-all phrase "disrespect for cultural sensitivities" might be better understood when viewed from the reality of a white man confronted by an aggressive band of tribesmen brandishing weapons and threatening violence, when Mr. Romilly with characteristic clarity of view, says:

> unless large allowances are made for them by white men trading in their midst, that friendly relations are not likely to continue for long unimpaired. Many a white man has offended their prejudices and done so unconsciously but with serious results to himself. No allowance is made for him by the natives on the score of ignorance. They assume that he is as conversant with their customs and superstitions as they themselves are. Their reasoning faculties are not sufficiently acute to perceive that it is impossible he should be so till he has spent some years of his life amongst them, nor do they possess any abstract idea of justice as we understand the word. The lex talionis they understand, but even in enforcing this law, they would prefer two eyes for an eye and two teeth for a tooth.[117]

---

116 British New Guinea, Report for 1887, Special Commissioner, Melbourne 1888 p 35.
117 Ibid., p 36.

Chart 6

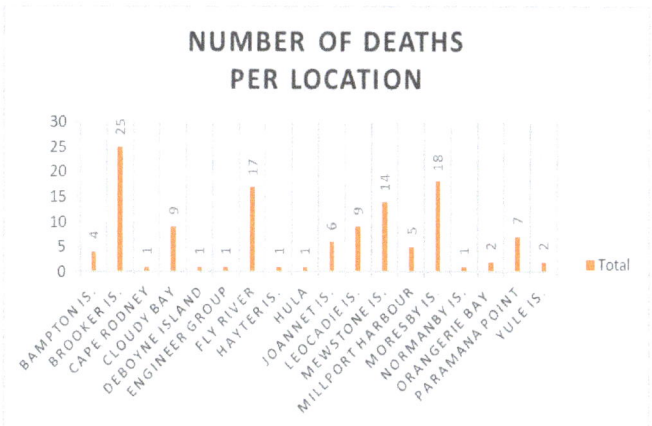

SEXUAL ABUSE OF PAPUAN WOMEN BY EUROPEANS.

Again, Mr. Romilly will do the honours and clear the air with some straight talking and clear thinking on the matter:

> 6. It is impossible, while on the subject of the causes which promote quarrels and bloodshed between the two races, to omit the mention of one fruitful cause of disorder and murder. I allude to the intercourse between white men and native women. The question has frequently been discussed before, but I think the tendency in such discussions has generally been to place the white man on too low a pedestal and the native woman on too high a one. To explain my meaning clearly, it will be necessary to say a few words about the position women hold in their tribe and the estimation in which they are held.
>
> We are apt to fall into the same mistake in our estimate of them as the natives do in their estimate of us. The intimacy of married life, as we understand it, among them does not exist at all. A woman after marriage is as much her husband's property as his spear or canoe is; she is his slave and must bear his ill-tempers and castigations without complaint. She bears him one child every three or four years, and her services are entirely at his disposal, whether he requires them for himself, or whether he requires them from a feeling of hospitality or profit, for another. She would have no voice in the matter. Virtue with her is generally compulsory, as any deviation from its path would bring her husband's anger upon her.

> In intercourse with white men, it is a matter of daily occurrence that husbands prostitute their wives for their own gain; nor, if the price previously arranged be paid, would any feeling of dishonour or dissatisfaction remain behind. Before marriage, the woman is her own mistress. The immorality of her life begins when she is a little child playing about the native villages with other children. When she is grown up, she would not of her own accord solicit white men, as she would be aware that her father or brother would deprive her of any profits which might accrue from such a proceeding. It is also probable that she prefers her own people. But she is frequently ordered by her relations to accept the solicitations of white men, and her future value, matrimonially, is not damaged. It is when white men desire to attain their ends without the intervention of the relations that claims for compensation are made. If they are refused, the quarrel not infrequently ends by the murder of the offending white man.[118]

In summation, the dominant feature in the settlement of British New Guinea that must be kept at the forefront of any consideration of colonisation is that there was no large-scale white settler land rush and the consequent dispossession, eviction and replacement of indigenous populations from their tribal homelands. Modern analysis of colonisation is usually predicated on the basis of white settlers invading and evicting indigenous natives from their homelands with military-style force. This did not happen in New Guinea in the geographical area and period of this study. British and Australian colonial interference, intrusion and involvement in British New Guinea were predicated on keeping out other colonial powers, controlling British subjects within the jurisdiction and protecting the indigenous natives within the jurisdiction. But before the reader responds, perhaps a little taste of Adam Smith might sweeten the pot:

> The discovery of America, and that of a passage to the East Indies by the Cape of Good Hope, are the two greatest and most important events recorded in the history of mankind. Their consequences have already been great... By uniting in some measure, the most distant parts of the world, by enabling them to relieve one another's wants, to increase one another's enjoyments, and to encourage one another's industry, their general tendency would seem to be

---

118 Ibid., p 36.

beneficial. To the natives, however, both of the East and West Indies, all the commercial benefits which can have resulted from those events have been sunk and lost in the dreadful misfortunes which they have occasioned. These misfortunes, however, seem to have arisen rather from accident than from anything in the nature of those events themselves. At the particular time when these discoveries were made, the superiority of force happened to be so great on the side of the Europeans that they were enabled to commit with impunity every sort of injustice in those remote countries. But nothing seems more likely to establish this equality of force than that mutual communication of knowledge, and of all sorts of improvements, which an extensive commerce from all countries to all countries naturally, or rather necessarily, carries along with it.

Each group of Europeans went to New Guinea for a purpose. The Royal Navy ruled the waves and spent its time policing the Western Pacific Islands. The London Missionary Society went to spread the gospel and save souls. Explorers and collectors went to discover and collect rare specimens and the traders and fishermen went to create wealth. From the above narrative, contact between the foreigners and the indigenous natives resulted in collisions. These collisions involved not only loss and damage to property but also loss of life. Within the narrative above, there is a collection of probable causes for these collisions. Taken as a whole, do they amount to a hypothesis? Or were they just a series of random results arising out of the innumerable collisions?

Speaking broadly, for a group of indigenous people who collectively practised headhunting and cannibalism, where the prey was another human being, perhaps, colonisation and the propagation of the Christian gospel may have been a worthy cause, even though there was a loss of life.

3

COMPARE AND CONTRAST

In the introduction to this book, I referred to my book *Bêche-de-mer and the Binghis*[119] and said that the original plan was to have included Aboriginals from the mainland of the colony, Pacific Islanders, Torres Strait Islanders, and the indigenous natives of British New Guinea in a study of marine incidents in Queensland waters and adjacent islands. However, the work became far too extensive. Even a book of 500 pages would not have adequately dealt with the subject material.

Bêche-de-mer and the Binghis dealt with Queensland coastal and reef waters where "it was found that two types of activity emerged from the data, Bêche-de-mer fishers and Other. The category Other covered a broad range of activities. However, irrespective of the activity, when a vessel within this group, for whatever reason, found themselves shipwrecked, windbound or with shore parties on the Queensland foreshore or coastal islands, they were attacked by Aboriginals domiciled at the place of anchor or landing."[120]

In the category Other, from 1859 to 1901, there were 20 marine incidents involving Aboriginals and Torres Strait Islanders. Indigenous Australians killed 50 white men and one Aboriginal, who were shipwrecked or shore parties.[121]

In the Bêche-de-mer industry, within the relevant period, 75 marine incidents occurred in which 124 persons were killed or murdered. The predominant causes of death were attacks by myall blacks and binghi crews. A further category of death was the drownings of binghi crews.[122]

---
119 BÊCHE-DE-MER and the BINGHIS by Paul Dillon, ISBN: 978-0-9946381-4-4, 2022 p 7.
120 Ibid., p 56.
121 Ibid., p 57.
122 Ibid., p 58. Myall blacks and binghi crews are Australian indigenous natives.

Number of Deaths by Cause

Race	Myall	Binghis	Others[123]	Total Killed
European/White	9	32	1	42
Asian	5	10	nil	15
Kanakas	4	5	5	14
Binghis	1	6	46	53

Graph 2 — Bêche-de-mer Industry (Queensland)

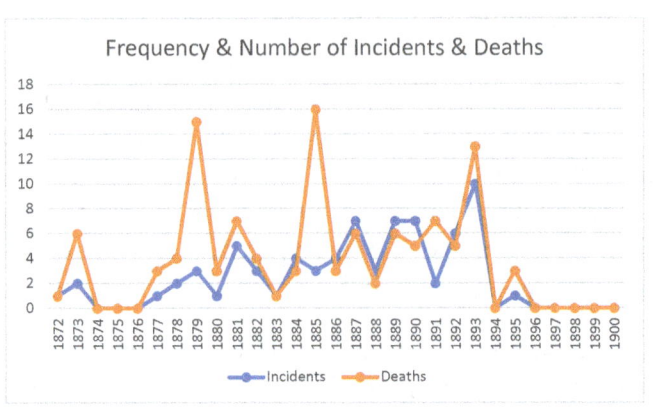

Graph 3 — Bêche-de-mer Industry (Queensland)

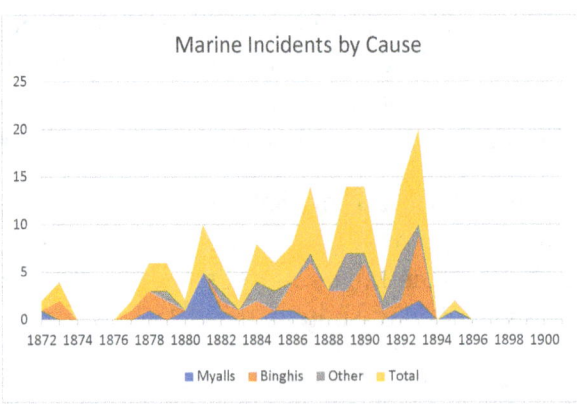

There were 95 marine incidents in Queensland waters and adjacent islands which involved mainland Aboriginals and Torres Strait Islanders. Arising out of these incidents, the number of deaths by race was as follows:

---

123 Others is a mixed-race category and it cannot be assumed that as a class they were exclusively white men and includes deaths by drowning or missing at sea.

Deaths from Marine Incidents involving Aboriginal and Torres Strait Islanders

Race	Number
White men	92
Aboriginal	54
Asian	15
Kanakas	14
Total	175

NEW GUINEA WATERS.

Papuan natives caused 124 European deaths[124] in 48 marine incidents. These non-Papuan deaths are identified as follows:

Deaths per each European Group[125]

Royal Navy	Missionary	Fishery	Trader	Explorer
nil	6	91	20	7

Chart 1

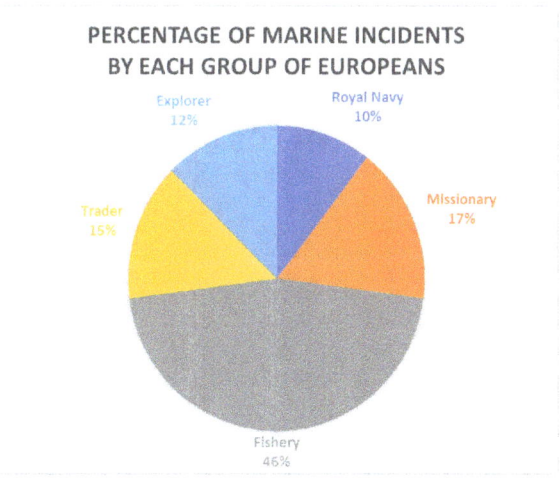

---

124 See pages 150-152 below.
125 Note European in this context may include non-whites acting as servants or agents of whites.

Both studies show that bêche-de-mer fishers were the most vulnerable group of Europeans in Queensland waters and New Guinea and adjacent island waters. The simple reason appears to be that they had the most frequent and intimate contact with each of the indigenous groups.

The reader needs to understand that there was a significant difference in the way the fishery was conducted in New Guinea waters. The fisher would visit each village and buy the dried bêche-de-mer from the indigenous native or enter into an exclusive contract with the villager to supply the fisher to the exclusion of all other fishers. Whereas in Queensland, the fisher was forced to employ Aboriginals as labourers to gather and process the fish, a far greater risk to the fisher.[126]

---

126 Toil, Travel, and Discovery in British New Guinea by Bevan, Theodore Francis, 1890, London: Kegan Paul, Trench, Trübner p 147.

4

POSTSCRIPT

There is not a lot of academic literature on the history of British New Guinea. The period under study is not noted for large white settler invasions of tribal homelands for economic exploitation. The frontiers of this colony might be described as missionary and trader. The reader needs to keep squarely in mind the difference between a trader frontier and a settler frontier. The settler is an invasive body seeking to enter and use tribal lands for economic purposes. The settler can be short-term like miners, or long-term settlers seeking to assert ultimately, exclusive title and sovereignty over the occupied land. I have used the term trader frontier because trader as a generic term includes any type of mercantile activity. For this chapter, trader includes the activity of pearlshell and bêche-de-mer fishing, harvesting, collecting and value-adding for the market.

The study as outlined above revealed that the largest group of foreign operators on the south-east coast and adjacent islands of New Guinea were traders and it was at this frontier that the largest number of marine incidents occurred involving Papuans, which often resulted in the death of the traders.

Alternate historiography has arisen in Australia, which postulates that white settlers invaded Australia and the indigenous people resisted with force when necessary; it is called Invasion history. Of the academic literature that exists on pre-colonial and colonial British New Guinea, John Mayo's *A Punitive Expedition in British New Guinea, 1886*[127] is perhaps the first in the modern era. However, Mayo has not adopted the rhetoric of the Invasion School or the Black Armband school of thought.

Mayo selected one incident, known as the Craig Massacre, to write a critique on. The article is defective as it does not give a context to the incident, nor does the author clearly state the political and legal background of the incident. He calls the reaction of the authorities to the murder of Craig and his crew, a punitive expedition, but does not define what a punitive expedition is. The definition of a punitive expedition per Stowell (1921) is:

> When the territorial sovereign is too weak or is unwilling to enforce respect for international law, a state which is wronged may find it necessary to invade the territory and to chastise the individuals who violate its rights and threaten its security.

However, Mayo, in describing the posse comitatus, gives a clear and accurate statement of the posse's instructions:

> Douglas instructed Forbes to go to Joannet Island to enquire into the circumstances of Craig's massacre. His 'main object' was to arrest the murderers and recover the arms and other stolen property, and he was authorised to make use of the best means at your disposal to accomplish this. You must, however, be careful not to expose your own life or lives of your party to any serious risk by following the natives into the jungle, where the odds would be against you.[128]

These instructions are not consistent with the definition of a punitive expedition. Forbes's party would be better described as a police operation. Forbes carried out his instructions from Douglas and reported to him the results of the posse. Douglas replied as follows:

> I feel satisfied that you carried out the instructions I gave you under circumstances of considerable emergency. The recovery of

---

[127] Mayo, John (1973) Punitive Expedition in British New Guinea, 1886, The Journal of Pacific History, 1973, Vol. 8, pp. 89-99. Mayo's footnotes have been checked, and footnote 16, Journal, Forbes Papers, Box 2.1, Fuller Collection, Bishop Museum (hereinafter Forbes Papers) should read Box 4.1.

[128] Ibid., Mayo p 93.

a portion of the arms as well as of the ammunition was one of the main objects of the expedition—and this you have effected.

4. I feel also bound to observe that it can never be my duty, or yours, to permit strife between neighbouring tribes. It may be necessary to visit offending natives with exemplary and judicial punishment. In the case now under discussion, the natives of Joannet doubtless richly deserved punishment, and I do not take exception to the fate which, at your hands, befell some of them, when the arms and ammunition were recovered, but the gratuitous burning of villages, even though those villages were deserted, I entirely disapprove of.[129]

Mayo's conclusions were as follows:

However, administrative policy remained a matter of trial and error, taking little or no consideration of native custom. It was based on the principles that the Government would protect native rights of life and property, and, more obviously, that the native peoples must realize that Government rules had to be obeyed. Punitive expeditions were a rough, ready, contradictory, undiscriminating and inefficient method of enforcing this 'policy'. But they were probably inevitable, considering the Protectorate's inability to sustain its officials in the field for long or give them sufficient support, and the inadequacy of the officials themselves.[130]

Mayo's conclusions are meaningless. He is careless with the use of technical words such as punitive. Douglas was endeavouring to inflict retributive punishment on the Papuans for killing white men, where no blame could be attached to the white man's behaviour.

The next scholarly work is *Black, White and Gold Goldmining in Papua New Guinea 1878–1930* by Hank Nelson.[131] Mr. Nelson describes his book as:

This book is about encounters between Papua New Guineans and

---

129 Griffith, Samuel & Forbes, Henry O & Douglas, John & Gillies, Duncan. (1887). Massacres in British New Guinea: (correspondence respecting, and report of special commissioner upon) Retrieved January 26, 2023, from http://nla.gov.au/nla.obj-3105134958 HC Command Paper C. 5883 p 128.
130 Ibid., Mayo p 99.
131 First published 1976 by The Australian National University, http://doi.org/10.22459/BWG.07.2016

miners from the first 'rush' in 1878 until 1930, four years after the alluvial miners finally found 'the big one'. This book also attempts to tell some of the history of the miners and Papua New Guinea communities, independent of their meetings. It is imperial history; not the history of colonial policy but of the behaviour of men on the frontier of empire.

Nelson's book is not relevant because it deals with the mining (gold) frontier, which commenced in June 1888 on the island of Sudest. However, Nelson includes in his narrative the Craig massacre, which occurred near the neighbouring island of Joannet (Pana Tinani). His contribution is as follows:

> The Craig 'massacre' of 1886, the most violent in a series of clashes between traders and villagers in south-east New Guinea, was followed by widespread demands for harsh reprisals. The traders' cry that now no white man would be safe in the area was all the more shrill because the Pana Tinani had taken fourteen rifles, four revolvers and ammunition from the *Emily* before they soaked her stored sails in kerosene and burnt her. The *Sydney Morning Herald* called on the government to shoot some islanders:
>
> Killing a few pigs and burning a few huts, which is the usual punishment inflicted by the British authorities upon the aboriginal murderers of Englishmen, will not be regarded as sufficient punishment for the death of Captain Craig and his crew.
>
> But as Queen Victoria's representative in Port Moresby, H.H. Romilly, pointed out, the government of the Protectorate of British New Guinea was uncertain of its powers to act and in the meantime 'the natives' could go on 'murdering away merrily'. A British man-of-war, *H.M.S. Diamond*, called at Pana Tinani but 'could do nothing'. Then Forbes fitted a Gatling gun to the schooner Coral Sea, hired Nicholas Minister and his cutter, the *Lizzie*, at £12 per week, collected a force of forty-five men from Wari Island and the eastern Louisiades, and sailed for Pana Tinani. A bêche-de-mer trader already in trouble for seizing island men for work and women for pleasure, Minister led a force of irregulars ashore, each man wearing a red badge to distinguish him from other islanders. The unofficial report said that when Minister returned next morning Forbes leaned over the rail and asked him if he had made contact with the man suspected of leading the attack on Craig. Minister replied, 'Yes, there's the bastard', and handed up a basket containing a head. In his official report, Forbes said Minister and his troop

shot Dagomi, a 'noted cannibal and robber' and father of the man who shot Craig, wounded some other men, burnt three villages and recovered guns and ammunition. The Pana Tinani retreated into dense scrub from where they fired guns on the government party. He banned foreign traders from Sudest and Pana Tinani.[132]

The difficulty with Nelson's work is that he does not footnote his work, but rather at the end of each chapter outlines what source material is available to the interested reader. Hardly satisfactory, but that is the nature of the book. Nelson does not in this book appear to be affected by the teachings of the Black Armband school of thought.

In 1998, Wayne Fife published *The Bampton Island Murders: Exploring the Human Face of Colonialism in Early Papua* in the Journal of the Polynesian Society.[133] This article is ostensibly about the Bampton Island murders. However, it is in reality an attempt to assess what I have called the missionary frontier in British New Guinea. On 1 December 1872, the London Missionary Society placed two teachers and their wives on Bampton Island to advance the aims and goals of the Society. On or about March 1873, it was found that the Brampton Islanders had murdered the teachers and their wives. The motive for the killings was robbery, and the taking of the teachers' property.

Fife attempts an extensive analysis of the situation, principally, by canvassing Captain Moresby's reaction to the conditions he found the Society's teachers in during his cruise of the Torres Strait and New Guinea coastal waters, with particular reference to the Redscar Bay missionary station. Fife's conclusions are:

> In my opinion, the native teachers and their wives on Bampton Island were victims of colonial hubris. Their deaths came about as a result of the particular kind of relationship that existed between the L.M.S. directors, the on-site British missionaries, native teachers and local peoples. The dangerous situations in which native teachers worked were an intrinsic aspect of these relationships. In their

---

132 Ibid., Nelson pp 13-14.
133 Fife, Wayne (1998) The Bampton Island Murders: Exploring the Human Face of Colonialism in Early Papua. The Journal of the Polynesian Society, vol. 107, no. 3, pp. 263–86.

role as shock troops, they took up the most vulnerable positions, acting as a buffer for the development of a British and Papuan connection. The Bampton incident cannot be taken in isolation and attributed to a few individuals or a local set of circumstances alone, even if these may prove to be the immediate triggers of the event. It must be looked upon in the light of the deaths of all the other Pacific evangelists in the New Guinea mission over the last several decades of the 1800s. When looked upon this way, we can see that the Bampton Island murders, like the later Kalo massacre and all of the other deaths and sufferings of the native teachers and their families, are about the relations of colonialism itself and the particular places of "native teachers" within that new social order. There is another understanding that we can reach from this material. The outcome of this case could have been significantly different. If Captain Moresby, for example, had publicly pressed his claims of missionary incompetence earlier or formally made them known to those who had the power to press for British government action.[134]

I don't know what Fife means when he says colonial hubris. Is he speaking of Anglo-Saxon chauvinism? He does not discuss the ethics of recruiting schooled natives to proselytise ignorant bush blacks. He merely calls the Society's teachers shock-troops as if that were a meritorious piece of scholarly perspicacity. Perhaps a comparison with the janissaries might have been more apt, or to recall the adage, to set a thief to catch a thief. Furthermore, it is anachronistic to suggest that a nineteenth-century officer of the Royal Navy should act as a modern-day whistle-blower. Fife's fatal flaw is that he failed to include and address Mr. A. Musgrave's paper, *Memorandum on the Mortality amongst Polynesian Teachers of the London Mission Society in British New Guinea, and the Alleged Dangerous Unhealthiness of the Territory*.[135]

The following incidents are outside the scope of the book. However, they need to be included because they belong within the general narrative of white Anglo-Australian colonial rule in New Guinea and its adjacent islands. The two incidents are the massacre of the Rev. James Chalmers and party at Goaribari Island, Western District, and the Nakanai massacre on the north coast of New

---

134 Fife, Wayne (1998) p 283.
135 British New Guinea, Report for 1888, Queensland 1889, Appendix E, pp 18-27.

Britain 120 miles from Rabaul. Chalmers and his party were killed in 1901 and the Nakanai incident in 1926.

The Nakanai incident was the subject of an article by Patricia O'Brien which was published in the journal, Australian Historical Studies in 2012.[136] The article does not refer to the murder of Rev. Chalmers and party of 1901.[137] She adopted the modern approach to writing Australian colonial history as outlined and prosecuted by Henry Reynolds and others. O'Brien says:

> Over recent decades, Australian historiography has focused squarely upon colonial violence, particularly in the form of collective punishment on Australia's pastoral frontiers. A number of Australia's most respected historians have convincingly demonstrated how endemic collective punishment was on Australia's frontiers and how frontier violence was a critical historical measure of Australia's political, social and cultural constitution. Yet these studies of violence and collective punishment have largely been confined within Australia's national borders. Pacific historians have also analysed violence in Australia's colonial contact with Pacific peoples, providing either a basis for Australia's colonial history in the Pacific generally, or New Guinea in particular. Through investigations of corporeal and capital punishments, labour indenturing and its multiplicity of abuses, sexualised violence and discriminatory juridical practices, these historians have variously shown the centrality of these forms of violence to Australia's colonial history with the Pacific Islands and its inhabitants. However, their analysis has not extended to punitive expeditions. Also, both groups of historians have largely operated in isolation from one another.[138]

In the above article, O'Brien mentions the phrase, machine gun, 18 times, as if it was emblematic of colonial rule and white aggression towards indigenous natives. The article is a rambling piece of prose with the monotonous refrain of punitive expeditions here, there and everywhere, echoing down the halls of leftist

---

136 Patricia O'Brien (2012): Reactions to Australian Colonial Violence in New Guinea: The 1926 Nakanai Massacre in a Global Context, Australian Historical Studies, 43:2, 191-209.
137 See: Patricia O'Brien (2009) Remaking Australia's Colonial Culture? White Australia and its Papuan Frontier 1901–1940, Australian Historical Studies, 40:1, 96-112, DOI: 10.1080/10314610802663043.
138 Op. cit. O'Brien (2012), p 191. This is a classic Black Armband Brigade beat-up.

academia.

The Rev. James Chalmers and party incident was the subject of an article by Dario Di Rosa which was published in the Journal of Colonialism & Colonial History in 2017.[139] Di Rosa quoted from O'Brien's article above. Di Rosa concluded:

> In 1904, when the Possession was still a British colony but the transition to an Australian administration was being debated, the (Australian) administrator failed to maintain control of his troops and used dishonourable practices to seize at least one of the "culprits" accused of the original killings, thus undermining the authority and integrity of the colonial state. In an era when Australia was becoming a colonial power in the Pacific, unrestrained violence came to be considered a serious threat to the honour of the state and its duties toward its colonial subjects, marking in Australian public discourses a difference from the supposed "British character" of earlier colonialism.[140]

Both incidents were covered by Chris Ballard and Bronwen Douglas in their article "Rough Justice:" Punitive expeditions in Oceania.[141] Their article was an attempt to focus on what they saw as frontier violence in Oceania and then to portray the violence in a way that suggested the colonial power was the aggressor while the indigenous native was the victim of a thoroughly gratuitous military action of suppression and reprisal.

The Chalmers incident and the Nakanai incident were within the jurisdiction of the municipal criminal law of British New Guinea and the Territory of New Guinea, respectively. Each incident was a police action to arrest and bring before the courts the indigenous natives alleged to have murdered white men.[142] Ballard and Douglas describe the incidents as follows:

> However, a punitive expedition might have been sanctioned at

---

139 Rosa, D.D. (2017). A Lesson in Violence: The moral dimensions of two punitive expeditions in the Gulf of Papua, 1901 and 1904. Journal of Colonialism and Colonial History 18(1), doi:10.1353/cch.2017.0001.
140 Ibid., p 9.
141 Ballard, C., & Douglas, B. (2017). "Rough Justice:" Punitive expeditions in Oceania. Journal of Colonialism and Colonial History 18(1), doi:10.1353/cch.2017.0018.
142 Herald 4 November 1926 p 1.

the outset, official and public approval was often retrospective. "Civilized outrage" in response to the contronym of a "Native outrage" could just as swiftly be turned upon the agents of punishment. The public response to the punitive expedition to the Nakanai in 1926, which had been relabelled an "affray," precisely and possibly consciously echoed events two decades earlier in British New Guinea: Di Rosa draws a sharp distinction between the reception of the two reprisals for the Chalmers massacre against the Kerewo of Goaribari Island. Whereas the first was understood to be a punitive expedition, conducted on behalf of the state according to established norms, the second, which engaged in deception deemed to be dishonourable (thus directly undermining the moral basis for intervention), was dismissed as an "affray." This distinction had dire consequences for Christopher Robinson, leader of the second expedition, who committed suicide in anguish over the public indignation at his actions.[143]

THE MASSACRE OF REV. CHALMERS AND PARTY

Thursday Island, 22 April 1901. The LMS schooner *Niue* anchored off the creek near Risk Point on Goaribari Island, near the mouth of the Omita River, in the eastern part of the western district of BNG. On the 8th instant, a party consisting of the Rev. Oliver Tomkins, in charge of the LMS's mission in Torres Straits, James Walker, a half-caste native of Torres Strait, together with the Rev. James Chalmers and nine mission students (natives of this district) and the chief of Akewai village left the *Niue* for the small creek, saying they would return in half an hour for breakfast. The *Niue* remained for the whole of the day, and that night. The vessel had in the meantime been surrounded by numerous canoes full of natives, who boarded and stripped her of everything in the shape of tanks, clothes, and trade. As the party had not returned, the vessel got up sail and cruised around the island, but could see or hear nothing of the party. The captain therefore determined to return to Daru and report what appeared to be a terrible massacre.[144]

---
143 Ballard & Douglas, (2017) p 6.
144 Telegraph 22 April 1901 p 2.

It was described by Kemeri:

> The signal for a general massacre was given by knocking simultaneously, from behind, both Messrs. Chalmers and Tomkins on the head with stone clubs. This was performed, in the case of the former, by Iake of Turotere; in that of the latter by Arau-u of Turotere. Kaiture, of Dopima, then stabbed Mr. Chalmers in the right side with a cassowary dagger; then Mururoa cut off his head; and Ema cut off Mr. Tomkins' head. They both fell senseless at the first blow of the clubs. All the heads were immediately cut off. We, however, lost one man, Gahibai, of Dopima. He was running to knock a big man [note this must be Naragi, chief of Ipisia) on the head, when the latter snatched a stone club from a man standing near and killed Gahibai. He (Naragi) was, however, immediately overpowered. The other boys were too small to make any resistance. In the meantime, the people in canoes left at the *Niue* returned to shore, after looting her of all the tomahawks, &c. This party was led by Kautiri, of Dopima. Finding the party on shore dead, it was determined to go back to the *Niue* and kill those on board. However, the *Niue* got underweigh and left. Then Pakara, of Aimaha, called out to all the people to come and break up the boat, which had been taken right inside the creek, it being high water. This was done, and the pieces were divided amongst people from the various villages. Directly, the heads had been cut off the bodies, some men cut up the bodies and handed the pieces over to the women to cook, which they did, mixing the flesh with sago. They were eaten the same day. Gebai has got Mr. Chalmers' head at Dopima, and Mahikaha has got Mr. Tomkins' head at Turotere. The rest of the heads are divided among various individuals.

The Administrator, Sir George Le Hunte, immediately organised an expedition consisting of several Europeans and 40-armed constabulary, which arrived at Goaribari Island on 2 May 1901 in the Government yacht *Merrie England*, accompanied by the *Ruby*, a launch. The s.s. *Parua* was sent by the Queensland Government with a small party of soldiers, to assist Lieutenant Brown and 10 men of the local Artillery Battery. When the boats reached land at the villages of Dopima and Turotere, the natives fired arrows at them; the signal to attack was therefore immediately given, and the boats' crews instantly opened fire with their rifles. The natives fled, and the punitive party occupied the villages. It was estimated that thirty-four of the natives were killed during these operations. After burning a number of dubus,[145] destroying 120 of the fighting canoes, and holding a funeral service in memory of the missionaries, the punitive expedition left Goaribari on 6 May 1901 with one prisoner, Kemeri.

The Administrator, Sir George Le Hunte, returned a second time to Goaribari Island from 1 to 6 March 1902. Prisoner Kemeri vanished. To gain the natives' confidence, on landing, Le Hunte promised he would take no action against them. He asked for the ringleaders to be handed over and the skulls of Chalmers and Tomkins returned. Only Chalmers' skull was returned. The ringleaders were about the place but Le Hunte would not take them, as the natives would see it as an act of treachery since he had given his word no harm would come to them.

The Acting-Administrator, Judge C. S. Robinson, Chief Judicial officer, visited Goaribari Island in the *Merrie England*, Captain R. H. Harvey, with Mr. E. Rothwell as Chief Officer, arriving there on 5 March 1904. Robinson was accompanied by the Resident Magistrate for the Division, with his party of seven native policemen, and by the Commandant of the Armed Native Constabulary with thirty-two native policemen, half of whom were raw recruits. On 6 March, while the ship was lying at anchor between the mainland and Goaribari Island, numerous natives, variously estimated as high as 600, came out to the vessel in their canoes. They seemed to have more confidence than the day before. Some of them came on board to trade with the crew, native weapons being bartered for tobacco, knives, etc. Iake was induced to come on board; Ema had been near the ship in his canoe but went back to shore. Shortly after the natives came on board, Iake and others were seized. The native police fired on the natives firing arrows at the ship from their canoes; the Acting-Administrator, the officers and the crew were also firing on the natives. Several natives were killed or wounded and retreated at once. In a few minutes, the firing ceased.

---

145 The longhouses of fighting men made of sago-palm.

The report of the Royal Commission (Judge Murray) appointed to inquire into the circumstances attending the affray at Goaribari Island British New Guinea, on 6 March 1904, was tabled in the House of Representatives on 13 September 1904. The findings of the Commission were, inter alia:

> Unequivocal treatment of savages necessary to retain their confidence, quite as much as the scrupulous execution of threats.
>
> Whole course of action condemned.
>
> The fault lies with the Judge (Mr. Robinson), but it is one of over-zeal and want of judgment.
>
> Firing by the Judge at retreating natives was inexcusable, unless, in charity, it be ascribed to temporary loss of self-control due to excitement.[146]

The Rev. E. Baxter Riley, writing to Mr. Thomas Pratt, representative of the London Missionary Society in Sydney, said that the *Merrie England* had been to Goaribari Island, and returned two natives, named respectively Iaki and Kauko, who had been arrested by order of Judge Robinson, the late Administrator, for being concerned in the murders. The natives had been in gaol at Port Moresby and were liberated on February 18, 1905. Five other men were detained at Daru, on account of the island being quarantined through the existence of whooping cough. Before leaving for home, they were requested to hand over to the Government the skull of the late Mr. Tomkins. This request was complied with, and it was in the possession of Mr. Riley at Daru. A native at Dopima, a village on the island where the massacre took place, assured the Government officer that the skull was the genuine one, and the authorities were satisfied that this was the case. It was found upon examination of the skull that the Rev. Mr. Tomkins was not clubbed, as was at first supposed. There was no fracture, and the skull was perfectly sound. After Mr. Chalmers was clubbed, Tomkins, with a few of the Kiwai (Fly River) boys, made for the whaleboat at top speed,

---

146 Australia. Parliament issuing body, author. (1904). Report of the Royal Commission on the affray at Goaribari Island, British New Guinea on the 6th of March 1904: together with the proceedings, minutes of evidence, and appendices Retrieved November 27, 2022, from http://nla.gov.au/nla.obj-2772887973

POSTSCRIPT

and, whilst running, was shot with arrows in the back, and, as he turned, in the chest, after which he was overpowered.[147]

My analysis of the Chalmers incident is as follows:

> In 1901, Chalmers, with reckless disregard for his own safety and the safety of his party, accepted an invitation from an unknown tribe and went to their island where they were murdered, and subsequently eaten by the offending tribe. The tribe then attacked Chalmers's ship and looted the ship but allowed it to leave the island.
>
> The Administrator of the colony, together with his police force, visited the island to investigate the matter and was attacked by the offending tribe. The police were ordered to fire on the tribe and a number were killed. The authorities then withdrew.
>
> The following year, 1902, the Administrator, together with police, revisited the offending tribe. A truce was called to inform the tribe that the heads of the two white men (Chalmers and Tomkins) had to be returned and the principal offenders had to surrender to police. One skull was returned, nothing else. The tribe (Dopima and Turotere) was then informed that "we have not made friends or done with them yet."
>
> In 1904, Robinson, the current Administrator, together with police, returned to the island to arrest the offending tribesmen. On arrest, the tribesmen resisted, and they were aided and abetted by other tribesmen firing arrows at the police, who returned fire, killing several tribesmen. The arrestees were transported to Port Moresby for trial.
>
> On 20 June 1904, Christopher Robinson, acting Administrator, killed himself by a gunshot wound to the head at Government House, British New Guinea and wrote as follows:
>
> To sum up, I was of the opinion, and am of the opinion still, that the firing was both justifiable and necessary. I think now that in the excitement which prevailed a good many more shots were fired than would have been if everyone who took part had remained cool and collected, but there are few who can remain unaffected by the excitement and confusion which naturally prevail under circumstances such as I have attempted to describe.[148]

---

147 Daily Telegraph 21 March 1905 p 4.
148 Op. cit. Report of the Royal Commission on the affray at Goaribari Island, British

A Royal Commission inquired into the matter. The commissioner did not discuss or examine whether the actions of Robinson and the police were within the laws of the colony but found the method or policy of Robinson was immoral in having lured the offending tribesmen onboard his ship for trade purposes and then arresting them. Police duplicity or treachery was not permissible in dealing with rude and uncivilised indigenous natives. If Robinson had given evidence before the Royal Commission, he may have been able to persuade them that he was within the law by arresting a fugitive from the law and that police were allowed or given wide latitude in bringing fugitives to justice.

THE NAKANAI MASSACRE

The League of Nations required a Mandatory power to present an annual report on the territory to the Permanent Mandates Commission of the League of Nations. At 11 a.m. on 23 June 1927, Sir Joseph Cook appeared for the government of Australia before the Permanent Mandates Commission concerning the administration of the mandated territory of New Guinea, report for 1926. The Nakanai incident was introduced in the following way.

> The Chairman noted that in the report no reference had been made to the troubles in the gold fields of New Guinea during the latter part of 1925. The *Times* of 11 January 1927, as stated that the mandatory Power had not been altogether satisfied with the way in which General Wisdom, the Governor General had handled the situation, more particularly with regard to the use of a machine gun which had resulted in the death of a certain number of natives.
>
> Sir Joseph Cook said that full information regarding these incidents would be included in the next report. They had not been included in the present report in view of the fact that the incidents had occurred in November 1926. He was, however, in the position to give the following information:

New Guinea on 6 March 1904, paragraph 47.

POSTSCRIPT

Murder of white men by natives at Nakanai, Territory of New Guinea.

In November 1926, four white men were killed by natives at a place called Nakanai on the island of New Britain. The administrator reported that, prior to this incident, four gold prospectors had entered the Nakanai area in search of gold or other minerals. One of the party was left at a base, while the others penetrated further inland. The man left at the base was attacked by the natives and wounded, but the whole of the party reached the coast and returned to Rabaul. Although aware of these facts, five other prospectors with one of the original party entered the area, apparently eager to secure claims. Whilst camped in a village, they also were attacked by natives, four of them being killed. Upon the Administration learning of this occurrence, an expeditionary party was organised and sent out, under the control of the District Inspectors to arrest the murderers.

When the equipment of the party including a machine gun, came under the notice of the Minister, he issued a direction to the Administrator that the gun was not to be used unless some grave emergency arose that rendered its use necessary for the protection of the lives of the members of the expedition, that it was upon no account to be used for purposes of aggression, and that the objects of the expedition were to be confined to the arrest of the murderers and natives implicated in the murders and the establishment of an advance post and were not to extend in any way to reprisals.

Upon its arrival in the Nakanai area, the expedition found its advance opposed by a body of hostile natives armed with native weapons and occupying a high ridge. As the only approach to the position occupied by these natives was through a steep and narrow path, some difficulty was experienced and the machine gun was used to provide covering fire to enable the expedition to advance. It was again found necessary, on the following day, to resort to the use of arms to ward off an attack made upon the expedition by the natives. The natives, on realising that they were unable to overpower the expedition, deserted their villages and took to the bush. The energies of the expedition were then directed to getting into touch with the fugitives through the medium of friendly natives in the neighbouring and undisturbed areas and inducing them to return to their villages so that efforts might be made to discover the actual murderers and those implicated in the murders.

After spending some days on this work, the expedition returned to Rabaul and was replaced by a smaller party. By the end of December, the majority of the fugitives had returned to their villages, and the names of the principal offenders had been obtained. Normal conditions now prevail, and the murderers have been identified and are awaiting transport to Rabaul. An administrative post has been established in the area to consolidate the influence gained and of bringing the natives under full control. In repulsing the attacks made upon the expedition, unfortunately, 18 natives were killed. The reasons for the attacks upon the white men have not yet been established but the indications are that the murders were indirectly due to the ill-treatment of the natives by certain native police and carriers who accompanied a Patrol Officer on a trip to the Nakanai area shortly before the incidents related took place. If any such ill-treatment occurred and was not punished on the spot, the natives would he prone to believe that it met with the approval of the officer, and this would engender a feeling of hostility towards all white men. The Patrol Officer in question is not now in the service of the Administration, but investigations are proceeding with the object of determining whether there was any ill-treatment of the natives at the hands of native police and carriers, and if so, of bringing the offenders to trial. As there has been some misapprehension as to the locality in which these disturbances occurred, it may be mentioned that Nakanai is on the island of New Britain, about 100 miles from Rabaul and that the happenings there are not in any way connected with the goldfields, which are in the Morobe District on the mainland of New Guinea.

Continuing, Sir Joseph Cook said: It seems to me that has a bearing upon one point which is so often being urged here, as to the necessity of proceeding quickly at the outbreak of a disturbance. Here is an instance of what occurs if you are not very careful in doing that very thing. It seems that the trouble arose not because the prospectors were prospecting for gold but because this patrol officer was trying to open a new section and the native police who were with him in some way interfered with the natives with the result that will be seen.

The Chairman thanked Sir Joseph Cook for this information and expressed the hope, on behalf of the Commission, that the incident would give rise to no unfortunate circumstances. He had only asked the question because it had appeared from the press that the Government of Australia had considered the use of the machine gun to have been excessive.

Sir Joseph Cook would emphasise the difficult nature of the country, which was very mountainous and full of ravines thus making

POSTSCRIPT

penetration difficult.[149]

Rabaul, 17 November 1926. The Nakanai massacre occurred in the district near Talasea on the north coast of New Britain, 120 miles from Rabaul. The District Officer and two assistants with about 30 police proceeded to the scene only to find a party of six prospectors, Messrs. N. T. Collins, B. I. Marlay, L. A. Fischer and D. Page were killed, while Britten and Nickols escaped. District Officer (D. O.) Taylor returned to Rabaul and reported the murders and recommended that a large force was necessary to cope with the hostile natives of that district.

Intense excitement was aroused in Rabaul over this affair and the repeated attacks on Europeans in this district. A Citizens' indignation meeting was held which passed a resolution and sent a deputation urging the Administrator to allow citizen volunteers to accompany the official expedition, to ensure adequate forces to subdue the district. Permission for this was granted, and a force was organised at once under the command of Lieutenant Colonel John Walstab, together with the District Officer, two assistants and about sixty police. There were about fourteen armed citizen volunteers in the party. They were subjected to a night attack under cover of a rainstorm but the attackers were driven off. Three were shot dead and a number were wounded. The report stated that there was evidence in numerous villages of complicity in the massacre. All such villages were burnt and their gardens destroyed.[150]

Arising out of the incident 14 natives were arrested and tried. They were found guilty and sentenced to death. However, their sentences were commuted to 15 years imprisonment.[151]

---

149 R54-1-60241-16466-Jacket1, Permanent Mandates Commission - Minutes of the meetings, 11th session, 20 June. 1927 (Creation).
150 Papuan Courier 19 November 1926 p 5. Cairns Post 16 December 1926 p 5. Idriess, Ion L. The Trouble at Nakanai, The Wide World Magazine; London Vol. 69, (Apr 1932): 23-35.
151 Herald 12 July 1927 p 5. Daily Telegraph 25 November 1927 p 2, Newcastle Morning Herald and Miners' Advocate 25 November 1927 p 5.

TABLE 1 — MARINE INCIDENTS

Ship	Date	Location	Event	Remarks
	June 1871	Corn wallis Is. (Dauan Is.)	Native staff threatened	LMS staff, conflicting versions
	March 1873	Bampton Island	2 teachers & wives killed	LMS staff, no provocation
HMS Basilisk	7 May 1874	Caution Point east end BNG	Threatened attack	R.N. official cruise, unprovoked
HMS Basilisk	8 May 1874	Traitor's Bay	Attack on officers	R.N. official cruise, unprovoked
Ellen gowan	8-18 Dec 1875	Fly River	Several attacks on vessel	LMS, unprovoked
Neva	5 & 29 June, 18 Aug 1876	Fly River	Attacks on vessel	D'Albertis, unprovoked
Mayri	September 1876	Yule Island	Natives kill 2 white men	LMS Dr James & Mr Thorngren, collecting
Neva	1 June to 19 Nov 1877	Fly River	Several attacks on vessel	D'Albertis, unprovoked
Bertha	December 1877	Hoop Iron Bay	Attack on water party	LMS unprovoked
Mayri	28 Dec 1877	South Cape	Capt. Dudfield speared	LMS unprovoked
	February 1878	Brooker Island	Natives kill 21 of Red-lich's crew	Bêche-de-mer station, destroy stn
	May 1878	Keppel Point	Attack on Rev. J Chalmers	LMS unprovoked
Pride of the Logan	July 1878	Keppel Point	Natives attack shore party	Bêche-de-mer fishers
Annie	July 1878	Keppel Point	Natives attack shore party	Bêche-de-mer fishers

POSTSCRIPT

Voura	November 1878	Brooker Island	Killed Ingham, Isles, & 2 Chinese	Recovering Redlich's gear.
Minnie Low	November 1878	Cloudy Bay	Killed Irons & Willis	Cedar getters
Oscar	3/3/1879	Cape Rodney	Killed 1 crew	Bêche-de-mer station
	March 1879	Dedele Point	Attack on search party	Bêche-de-mer fishers Re Irons
Chinese Junk	May 1879	Dufaure Island	Chinese crew attacked	Bêche-de-mer fishers
Ellen gowan	June 1879	Cloudy Bay	Attack shore party	LMS unprovoked
Pride of the Logan	29/9/1879	Cloudy Bay	Killed 1 white wo-man, 3 white men, 3 Chinese	Bêche-de-mer station
Wong Hing	1/1/1880	Real Island (Panasia)	Attack vessel, driven off	Bêche-de-mer fishers Chinese
Sin O Ney	31/7/1880	Paramana Point	7 Chinese killed	Bêche-de-mer fishers
Annie Brooks	September 1880	Mewstone Island	Killed 7 whites & 7 Chinese	Bêche-de-mer fishers
	12/10/1880	Moresby Island	Killed 7 French men	Naturalists seeking specimens
Prosperity	October 1880	Leocadie Island	Killed 9 Chinese	Bêche-de-mer fishers
Pride of the Logan	24/7/1882	Bootless Inlet	Killed 1 native, 1 wounded	Bêche-de-mer, stealing tobacco
Tavioni	October 1882	Fly River	Crew of 17 killed, heads taken	Wreckage found in Fly River
Foi	27 May 1884	Mia Kassa River	Attack party, 1 wounded, Kerry	2nd *Age* exploration party
Fow Gow	17/8/1884	Hula	Killed 1 Chinese crew	Bêche-de-mer fishing
Wild Duck	27/9/1884	Cloudy Bay	White crew attacked	Bêche-de-mer fishing
Elibank Castle	23/12/1884	Engineer Group	Killed Reid	Copra trading
Marion	1884	Millport Harbour	Murdered Webb, wife & 3 blacks	Bêche-de-mer fishing
PTM	31/1/1885	Deboyne Island	Murdered F Gerret	Bêche-de-mer fishing
HMS Swinger	February 1885	Millport Harbour	Natives attacked a shore party	Royal Navy patrol
	22/2/1885	Hayter Island	Lumse killed	Bêche-de-mer

115

		Sept 1885	Hood Lagoon	Robbery of Rowan	Bêche-de-mer
Lalla Rookh		29/7/1885	Moresby Is	Killed Frier, 1 white, 2 kanakas, 1 AB	Bêche-de-mer fishing landed for water & firewood
Daisey		3/10/1885	Normanby Island	Captain F. Miller Killed	Bêche-de-mer fishing
		Oct 1885	Killerton Is.	Attack on Hunstein	Trader
Electra		1/1/1886	Round Head	Crew attacked	Exploration
Electra		January 1886	Round Head	Vessel plundered	Exploration
Marion		26 May 1886	Toulon Island	Vessel destroyed	Trader, copra
HMS Swinger		July 1886	St Aignan Island	Capt. Marx wounded	Royal Navy
Hector		3/9/1886	Gaba Gabuna Bay	C. Berlin attacked	Trader
Emily		16/9/1886	Joannet Island	Killed crew 3 whites, 5 Malays	Pearling Capt. Craig, vessel burnt by natives
Pride of the Logan		May 1887	Moresby Island	Vessel wrecked Chinese murdered	Bêche-de-mer fishing
Cecilia		July 1887	Orangerie Bay	Attacked by natives 2 killed	Trader landed for water & firewood

BIBLIOGRAPHY

Alexander, Gilchrist (1927) *FROM THE MIDDLE TEMPLE TO THE SOUTH SEAS,* John Murray, London.

Bach, John (1986) *The Australia Station: A History of the Royal Navy in the South West Pacific, 1821-1913,* UNSW Press, Sydney.

Ballard, C., & Douglas, B. (2017) *"Rough Justice:" Punitive expeditions in Oceania,* Journal of Colonialism and Colonial History 18(1), doi:10.1353/cch.2017.0018.

Bevan, Theodore Francis (1890) *Toil, travel, and discovery in British New Guinea,* Kegan Paul, Trench, Trübner, London.

Chalmers, James (1887) *Pioneering in New Guinea,* The Religious Tract Society, London.

Cilento, Raphael and Clem Lack (1959) *Triumph in the Tropics. A Historical Sketch of Queensland,* Historical Committee, Centenary Celebrations Council of Queensland, Brisbane.

D'Albertis, L. (1880) *NEW GUINEA: What I Did and What I Saw,* VOL. II. Sampson Low, Marston, Searle, & Rivington, London.

Fife, Wayne (1998) *The Bampton Island Murders: Exploring the Human Face of Colonialism in Early Papua.* The Journal of the Polynesian Society, vol. 107, no. 3, pp. 263–86.

Fitzgerald, C. C. Penrose (1897) *Life of Vice-Admiral Sir George Tryon, K.C.B.,* W. Blackwood and Sons, Edinburgh.

Gordon, Donald Craigie (1951) *The Australian frontier in New Guinea: 1870-1885,* Columbia University Press, New York.

Idriess, Ion L. The Trouble at Nakanai, The Wide World Magazine; London Vol. 69, (Apr 1932): 23-35.

Jinks, Brian (1973) *Readings in New Guinea History*, Angus & Robertson, Sydney.

Kinloch-Cooke, Clement (1887) *Australian Defences and New Guinea compiled from papers of Peter Scratchley*, Macmillan, London.

Lātūkefu, Sione (1989) Papua New Guinea: A Century of Colonial Impact, 1884-1984, National Research Institute and the University of Papua New Guinea.

Lovett, Richard (1899) *The History of the London Missionary Society, 1795-1895*, H. Frowde, London.

Mair, Lucy Philip (1970) *Australia in New Guinea*, Melbourne University Press, Melbourne.

Mayo, John (1973) *Punitive Expedition in British New Guinea, 1886*, The Journal of Pacific History, 1973, Vol. 8, pp. 89-99.

McCarthy, J K (1967) *Patrol Into Yesterday: My New Guinea Years*, F W Cheshire, Melbourne.

McIntyre, W. D. (1960) *Disraeli's colonial policy: The creation of the Western Pacific High Commission, 1874–1877*, Historical Studies: Australia and New Zealand Volume 9, Issue 35: 279-294.

Monckton, C. A. W. (1921) *Some experiences of a New Guinea resident magistrate*, J. Lane, London.

Moresby, John (1876) *Discoveries & Surveys in New Guinea and the D'Entrecasteaux Islands; a cruise in Polynesia and visits to the pearl-shelling stations in Torres Straits of H. M. S. Basilisk*, J. Murray, London.

Murray, John Hubert Plunkett, Sir (1912) *Papua: or, British New Guinea*, T. Fisher Unwin, London.

Nelson, Hank (1976) *Black, White and Gold Goldmining in Papua New Guinea 1878–1930*, ANU Press, Canberra.

Nelson, H. (1982) *Taim bilong masta — The Australian*

involvement with Papua New Guinea, ABC Books, Sydney.

O'Brien, Patricia (2009) *Remaking Australia's Colonial Culture? White Australia and its Papuan Frontier 1901–1940,* Australian Historical Studies, 40:1, 96-112, DOI: 10.1080/10314610802663043

O'Brien, Patricia (2012) *Reactions to Australian Colonial Violence in New Guinea: The 1926 Nakanai Massacre in a Global Context*, Australian Historical Studies, 43:2, 191-209.

Palmer, George (1871) *Kidnapping in the South Seas. Being a narrative of a three months' cruise of H.M. ship Rosario,* Edmonston and Douglas, Edinburgh.

Pitcairn, W. D. (1891) *Two Years Among the Savages of New Guinea,* Ward & Downey, London.

Price, A. Grenfell (1963) *The Western invasions of the Pacific and its continents: a study of moving frontiers and changing landscapes, 1513-1958,* Clarendon Press, Oxford.

Rosa, D.D. (2017) *A Lesson in Violence: The moral dimensions of two punitive expeditions in the Gulf of Papua, 1901 and 1904,* Journal of Colonialism and Colonial History 18(1), doi:10.1353/cch.2017.0001.

Romilly Hugh Hastings (1886) *The Western Pacific and New Guinea: notes on the Natives, Christian and Cannibal, with some account of the Old Labour Trade,* John Murray, London.

Scarr, Deryck (1967) *Fragments of Empire A History of the Western Pacific High Commission 1877-1914,* ANU Press, Canberra.

Thompson, Roger C (1980) *Australian imperialism in the Pacific: the expansionist era, 1820-1920,* Melbourne University Press, Melbourne.

Abbreviations

A. & P.	House of Commons, Accounts and Papers.
C	Command paper, UK Parliamentary Papers
GG	Queensland Government Gazette
HC	House of Commons
HL Deb	House of Lords Debate
HMS	Her Majesty's Ship
LA	Queensland Legislative Assembly
LC	Queensland Legislative Council
LMS	London Missionary Society
NAA	National Australian Archives
PMB	Pacific Manuscripts Bureau catalogue
PM	Police Magistrate
QSA	Queensland State Archives
RN	Royal Navy

www.ingramcontent.com/pod-product-compliance
Lightning Source LLC
Chambersburg PA
CBHW070400240426
43671CB00013BA/2578